Essentials of Teaching Academic Vocabulary

HOUGHTON MIFFLIN
ENGLISH FOR ACADEMIC SUCCESS

Averil Coxhead
Massey University, New Zealand

SERIES EDITORS

Patricia Byrd
Joy M. Reid
Cynthia M. Schuemann

Houghton Mifflin Company
Boston   New York

D0595251

Publisher: Patricia A. Coryell
Director of ESL Publishing: Susan Maguire
Senior Development Editor: Kathy Sands Boehmer
Editorial Assistant: Evangeline Bermas
Senior Project Editor: Kathryn Dinovo
Director of Manufacturing: Priscilla Manchester
Senior Marketing Manager: Annamarie Rice
Marketing Assistant: Andrew Whitacre

Cover graphics: LMA Communications, Natick, Massachusetts

Printed in the U.S.A.

Library of Congress Control Number: 2003110101

ISBN: 0-618-23014-9

123456789-EUH-09 08 07 06 05

Contents

Other resources available at www.college.hmco.com/esl/instructors

Preface

Patricia Byrd, Joy M. Reid, Cynthia M. Schuemann

The Houghton Mifflin English for Academic Success (EAS) series is a comprehensive program of student and instructor materials. For students, the series contains four levels of student language proficiency textbooks in three skill areas (oral communication, reading, and writing), with supplemental vocabulary textbooks at each level. For instructors and students, the series includes websites that support classroom teaching and learning. For instructors, four Essentials of Teaching Academic Language books, one for each skill area, provide helpful information for teachers new to teaching or to teaching a particular area for academic preparation. The four books in the Essentials series are:

- Coxhead, Averil. 2006. *Essentials of Teaching Academic Vocabulary.*
- Murphy, John. 2006. *Essentials of Teaching Academic Oral Communication.*
- Reid, Joy. 2006. *Essentials of Teaching Academic Writing.*
- Seymour, Sharon, and Laura Walsh. 2006. *Essentials of Teaching Academic Reading.*

Purposes of the EAS Series

The fundamental purpose of the EAS series is to prepare students who are not native speakers of English for academic success in U.S. college degree programs. By studying these materials, students in college English for Academic Purposes (EAP) courses will gain the academic language skills they need to be successful students. Additionally, students will learn effective strategies for participating in U.S. college courses.

The series is based on considerable prior research as well as our own investigations of students' needs and interests, teachers' needs and desires, and institutional expectations and requirements. For example, our survey research revealed what problems teachers believe they face in their classrooms, what teachers actually teach; who the students are, and what they know and do not know about the "culture" of U.S. colleges; and what types of "barrier exams" are required for admission at various colleges.

In addition to meeting student needs, the textbooks in the EAS series were created for easy implementation by teachers. First, because the books were all written by experienced ESL teachers, each textbook provides instructors with a range of practical support. Second, each textbook author worked with advisory groups made up of other classroom teachers, including adjuncts as well as full-time instructors. In addition to reviewing the various drafts of the book chapters, the advisory group members also field tested the materials with their own students to find out how the materials worked in class and to get student feedback for revisions. This team effort led to the development of authentic, effective, and appropriate materials that are easy to understand and teach. Additionally, each book has a website written by the author that contains helpful notes about teaching each chapter, an answer key, additional quizzes and other appropriate assessment tools, and handout and overhead masters that can be printed for class use.

The authors and editors were also aware that many instructors find themselves teaching courses in areas that are new or unfamiliar to them. To help teachers teach the areas covered by the EAS textbooks, a series of teacher reference books has been developed. These books present the *essentials* of teaching academic writing, academic reading, academic oral communication, and academic vocabulary. Written by scholar-teachers, these brief, well-organized Essentials books provide teachers with highly focussed help in developing their own knowledge and teaching skills.

Essentials Authors

As can be seen from these summaries of their work, the authors of the Essentials books are true scholar-teachers who bring considerable classroom knowledge to the teaching issues involved in English for academic purposes.

Averil Coxhead is the creator of the Academic Word List (AWL) that is widely used around the world as a basic tool in the development of student academic vocabulary. Now a faculty member in the School of Language Studies at Massey University in Palmerston North, New Zealand, Averil is an experienced classroom ESL teacher, particularly of English for Academic Purposes. She is, as well, a researcher on second language vocabulary development.

John Murphy is an associate professor in the Department of Applied Linguistics and ESL at Georgia State University in Atlanta, Georgia. In addition to his work with teachers in training, John has published numerous articles both theoretical and practical on issues in the teaching of oral communication. His highly practical strategies for teaching word syllable and stress analysis as a part of the vocabulary learning process are put into practice in the vocabulary and the oral communication textbooks in the EAS series.

Joy Reid, former TESOL president and now retired from the University of Wyoming, is currently teaching writing in the Foundations Unit at Maui Community College in Kahului, Hawaii. Joy's work on ESL writing is recognized internationally. In addition to her publications on the theory of second-language writing, she is the author and editor of many ESL composition textbooks. She brings forty years of teaching to the task of writing her *Essentials of Teaching Academic Writing*. She has also published ESL writing textbooks and resource books for teachers.

Sharon Seymour is the chair of the ESL Department at the City College of San Francisco, one of the largest ESL programs in the world. In addition to her administrative work, she is an experienced classroom teacher. While on sabbatical in 1997, Sharon studied the reading demands of courses often taken by ESL students at her college. Using the information from that study and from other published work on academic reading, she worked with her department faculty to revise their curriculum to better prepare students to be effective academic readers.

Her colleague Laura Walsh is an experienced classroom teacher who has studied the literature on second-language reading and writing both as part of her graduate study and as subsequent professional development. As the credit ESL assessment coordinator at City College, Laura coordinates the development, implementation, and validation of ESL placement and promotion tests. She played a primary role in revising the academic ESL curriculum. Together, Sharon and Laura bring to their *Essentials of Teaching Academic Reading* substantial knowledge of classroom teaching, of the needs of college students, and of strategies and activities for teaching academic reading.

Acknowledgments

I would like to thank David Hirsh and Angela Joe from Victoria University of Wellington, New Zealand, and John Bunting from Georgia State University, for their helpful comments and collegial support. Thank you also to Norbert Schmitt for permission to include the Vocabulary Level Test in this book.

Pat Byrd's knowledge of the field and sharp eye for detail helped at all stages of the book production. Joy Reid and Cynthia Schuemann provided expertise and enthusiasm also. Thank you also to the other writers in the series who answered questions and shared drafts.

Kathy Sands Boehmer, Susan Maguire, Evangeline Bermas and Elaine Hall were helpful and kind. They also (possibly accidentally) acquired a few words of New Zealand English along the way.

Thank you also to my family and friends who at times decided not to ask how the book was going. Many thanks also to my students who tried out activities, gave feedback, and shared what they thought about learning words.

Finally, to Paul Nation from Victoria University of Wellington, New Zealand: thanks, Sport.

Averil Coxhead

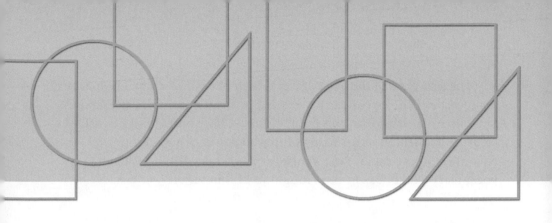

Introduction

General and Academic Vocabulary

1. What words do all learners need to know?
2. What is an academic vocabulary?
3. What is the Academic Word List?

Vocabulary is a central part of a language. The more words students know well and can use, the more meaning they can communicate in a wide variety of circumstances. This book focuses on teaching and learning academic vocabulary. It is specifically for teachers working with college-level students who need to develop their academic vocabulary to help them cope better with using English in demanding circumstances.

The book is divided into four parts.

- The first part outlines principles and ideas to think about before you start teaching words, such as finding out what students already know and principles and processes behind acquiring new words.
- The second part includes direct and indirect strategies for learning vocabulary, as well as using vocabulary notebooks and dictionaries.
- The third part is on developing academic vocabulary through skills-based classroom activities, that is, through reading, listening, speaking and writing.
- Finally, we will look at testing academic vocabulary, including some practical ideas on how and what to test.

The four parts of the book are all related but can be dipped into or read in any order. Where possible, I have tried to include examples or exercises.

There is a website for this book where we have posted links to useful websites and templates for many of this book's teaching activities. I encourage you to explore the website and to work with the academic vocabulary workbooks in this Houghton Mifflin series.

What Words Do All Learners Need to Know?

Before we begin to talk about academic vocabulary specifically, we need to consider the basic vocabulary all learners need to know. These words are called high-frequency vocabulary. Learners who plan to study at the college level need to be able to understand and use these words before they move on to learning academic words.

In any language there are words that occur more frequently than others. Compare the words in bold with the words in italics—which words do you think occur more frequently in everyday language than others?

> **of, a, the, do, is, we, to**
> *furthermore, hitherto, substantially*

The words in **bold** are used more often in general speaking and writing than **the** words in *italics*. **We** know this because **of** our daily experiences with language and our own patterns **of** use. As an example, you could look **to** see how many times **the** words in bold above occur in this paragraph. Because **the** bolded words occur very often, it **is** important that learners learn **to** recognise them when reading and listening. It **is** also important that students learn **to** use **the** words accurately and fluently in their speaking and writing.

Research tells us that there are approximately 2,000 word families[1] that are important because they make up the most frequent words in English.[2] In my study of academic vocabulary in written texts, I found that the first 2,000 words represented on average about 75 percent of the words in the texts I looked at.[3] The same list of 2,000 words might represent up to 90 percent of the words in a fiction story.

In summary, some words appear more frequently than others and those are the ones we should all try to teach first. I don't mean you should ask your learners in the first lesson to learn 2,000 words and their families.[4] I do mean that if you are choosing which words to work on in class, or highlighting words in passages, you should think about focusing on the high-frequency words first.[5] In other words, these words are worth the teaching and learning time and effort.

In Chapter 1 we will look at measuring how well students know the first 2,000 words. The key point is that learners need to have a good knowledge of these words because they give a good return for learning, no matter whether they continue to study at college or have other goals.

What Is an Academic Vocabulary?

Once learners are able to recognise and use the first 2,000 words of English, they need to move on to learning other vocabulary. If they plan to study at college, they will need to start learning to recognise and use words that occur regularly in their academic texts.[6] These words need to occur in many texts to be considered worthy of valuable class time and effort. These words are not technical or specifically linked to a subject area.

There are several key reasons why academic vocabulary is important to learners.

- Academic vocabulary is important because understanding and properly using this vocabulary allows students to be part of the academic community. If learners are not able to recognise or use this language, this can act as a kind of a barrier or 'lexical bar' to higher learning.[7]
- To be successful at university, learners need to be able to show that they can read, understand and respond clearly in writing and speaking to academic language and concepts.
- Vocabulary is a very important part of literacy.[8]
- Students will meet general academic words many times in their academic reading.[9]
- These words occur in a wide variety of subject areas.[10]

Academic vocabulary occurs mostly in academic texts.[11] This may seem like a simple thing, but it is important to remember. The short passage below comes from an introductory accounting textbook. The words in **bold** in the text are from the Academic Word List (AWL).[12]

Out of the 56 words in the passage, seven of them are in the AWL (roughly 12 percent of the text). I have counted words that are repeated twice (e.g., *financial*).

Conventions that help in the **interpretation** of **financial** information

To a large extent, **financial** statements are based on **estimates** and the application of accounting rules for recognition and **allocation**. In this book, we point out a number of difficulties with **financial** statements. One is failing to recognise the changing value of the dollar caused by inflation.[13]

Now compare the vocabulary in the passage above with this extract from the first part of this introduction. Out of the 54 words in this passage, two are in the AWL (roughly 3 percent of the text.)

The words in bold are used more often in general speaking and writing than the words in *italics*. We know this because of our daily experiences with language and our own patterns of use. As an example, you could look to see how many times the words in bold above **occur** in this **paragraph**.

You can see that the two passages above contain very different vocabulary. The number of words from the AWL is higher in the accounting text because it is academic in nature. The passage from this book is not particularly academic in nature, and contains a small number of academic words.

Newspapers also use many AWL words but generally not as often as academic texts do. The passage below is from a newspaper. Out of the 47 words in this passage, five are in the AWL (roughly 10 percent). This amount is unusually high. I conducted a study of one million words of newspaper text and found that the coverage of the Academic Word List was about 4.5 percent.

> ## E-MAIL TO HIT NEW ZEALAND PHONES
>
> A new hand-held **device** is expected to **revolutionise** the way people think about e-mail, according to Vodafone business marketing general manager Phil Patel. Vodafone is **releasing** a hand-held **device**, called a BlackBerry, that allows people to send and **respond** to e-mail messages.[14]

You can supplement classes with newspaper texts and be sure that learners are being exposed to academic vocabulary. If students follow the same news stories over the course of several weeks, they will gain repeated exposure to many words.[15]

Finally, learners have to engage with the words they are focussed on learning. If learners do not think about the words deeply, it will be harder to make the words 'stick'. In Part Three, we will look at activities you can use or adapt to your classroom that encourage your learners to engage with words from the Academic Word List (AWL).

What Is the Academic Word List?

The Academic Word List (AWL) is the result of my study of written academic texts.[16] The AWL has 570 word families and includes words such as *finance*, *purchase* and *research* as we have seen in the three passages above. Here are some key points about the AWL:

- The AWL is divided into 10 sublists. The first contains the 60 most frequent word families in the list. These 60 families account for approximately 3.5 percent of the words in a collection of written academic texts.[17] The second sublist contains the next most frequent 60 word families and so on. The sublists are based on frequency so that teachers and learners can focus initially on the AWL words that occur most often.
- The 60 words in the sublist provide teachers and learners with a solid number of words to work with. Sublist 10, however, has 30 words.
- The vocabulary books in this Houghton Mifflin series focus directly on the AWL and learning the words in context.

The AWL is a useful learning and teaching tool or guideline because it helps identify the words worth spending time on in class and means we do not have to rely so heavily on guess work or intuition.

Let's look at another passage of academic writing and examine the AWL words in it to see what we can find out about these words. The following is a passage from the same accounting textbook we looked at earlier. Take a look at the AWL words in **bold**. What features of the words do you notice?

> Of course, **investors** and **creditors** will want to do their own **analysis** of General Mills. This will **require** reading and **interpreting** the **financial** statements and calculating other **ratios**. However, the **analysis** will be meaningless unless the reader understands **financial** statements and generally accepted accounting **principles**, on which the statements are based.[18]

You might have noticed that there are many AWL words in the text. Of the 51 words in this passage, 10 are in the AWL (roughly 20 percent). Words such as *which*, *the*, and *however* are in the first 2,000 words of English.[19]

- The average figure for the AWL in written academic texts is about 10 percent.[20] The ratio of AWL words in this passage is higher than normal. My research found that the AWL words covered on average about 12 percent of the Commerce texts I worked with. Arts and Law texts averaged about 10 percent and Science covered just over 9 percent.[21]
- AWL words are more frequent in commerce texts because words like *financial*, *ratio*, and *analyze* are very common and are often repeated in academic textbooks on subjects such as accounting and economics.
- Of the words in the AWL, 80 percent come from Greek or Latin.[22] If your learners speak or understand a Romance language such as Spanish or French, they may well recognise many of the words in the AWL. If this is the case, you need to establish whether they know the words fluently and accurately in speaking and writing on academic topics. If your students come from non-Romance language backgrounds,

such as Mandarin, Arabic or Thai, they may not recognise and use the words as easily as the Romance background speakers.

In Part Three of this book, we will look at classroom-based activities that target the words in the AWL. For more on dealing with lower-frequency and subject-specific vocabulary, see Chapter 8.[23]

Now that we have looked at general and academic vocabulary, it is time to consider your learners, in terms of what they know and what they need to know in connection with academic vocabulary.

Endnotes

1. An example of a word family is *different* whose family includes *differ, difference, differences, differentiate, differentiation* etc.
2. West, M. 1953. *A general service list of English words.* London: Longman, Green and Co. and Nation, P. 2001. *Learning vocabulary in another language* on the Internet. There is more research being done in this area as people try to establish whether the current list is still usable even though it is quite old.
3. Coxhead, A. 2000. A new academic word list. *TESOL Quarterly 34*, (2); 213–238. You can find the AWL in Appendix 1 and on the website for this book at http://www.college.hmco.com/esl/instructors
4. A word family is basically all the words that are related to each other through form and meaning. For example, *make* including *made, making, makes, remake, remakes, remade, remaking* etc. For more on word families, see Chapter 1.
5. See Nation, P. 2001. *Learning vocabulary in another language.* Cambridge: Cambridge University Press, pages 13–17 for more on high frequency words.
6. By 'text' I mean the textbooks and other written and spoken communication on academic topics in academic style.
7. Corson, D. 1985. *The lexical bar.* Oxford: Pergamon Press.
8. Scarcella, R. 2002. Some key factors affecting advanced learners' development of literacy. In M. Schleppegrell and M. Colombi (eds.) *Developing advanced literacy in first and second languages.* Mahwah, New Jersey: Lawerence Erlbaum. Pages 209–226. Page 212.
9. Coxhead, 2000.
10. Coxhead, 2000.
11. Coxhead, 2000.
12. Coxhead, 2000.
13. Needles, B., Jr., M. Powers, & Crosson, S. 2005. *Principles of accounting.* Boston: Houghton Mifflin.

14. Mckenzie-Mclean, J. 2004. Email to hit NZ phones. *Manawatu Evening Standard*, Thursday 17 June, 2004. Retrieved on 18 June, 2004 from http://www.stuff.co.nz/stuff/print/0,1478,2943446a6022,00.html.

15. Schmitt, R. and Carter, R. 2000. The lexical advantages of narrow reading for second language learners, *TESOL Journal*. 9, 1: 4–9.

16. Coxhead, 2000.

17. Coxhead, 2000.

18. Extract from: Needles, B., Jr., M. Powers, & Crosson, S. 2005. *Principles of accounting*. Boston: Houghton Mifflin. Chapter 6, page 213.

19. West, M. 1953. *A general service list of English words*. London: Longman, Green and Co.

20. Coxhead, 2000.

21. Coxhead, 2000.

22. Coxhead, 2000.

23. If you still have worries about using vocabulary lists like the AWL in class, see Folse, K. 2004. *Vocabulary myths*. Ann Arbor: University of Michigan Press, pages 35–45 for an interesting and highly relevant discussion.

Part **1**

Essentials Before You Start Teaching Vocabulary

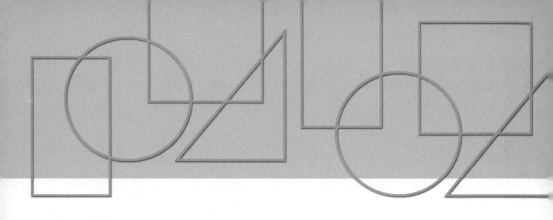

Chapter 1

Analyzing Your Students' Vocabulary

FEATURED IN THIS CHAPTER

- How can we find out how many words the students already know?
- What aspects of a word do learners need to know about?

In this chapter we will look at the words that learners need to know and how to find out how many words they already know so that we can make the most of learning opportunities in our college courses.

How Can You Find Out How Many Words Your Students Know?

It is important to find out quickly how many words your students already know and at what level. Before they move on to academic vocabulary, they need to have a solid working knowledge of the first 2,000 word families.[1]

In his book called *Learning Vocabulary in Another Language*,[2] Paul Nation has several tests of the first 1,000 words. These tests can give you a rough guide on the number of words your students know or understand in this first level. Tests that measure the learners' understanding of words when reading or listening are often called 'receptive' tests. Tests that measure how well learners can use words in writing or speaking are sometimes called 'productive' tests.

There are also receptive tests called The Vocabulary Level Tests.[3] You can find a version of these tests in Appendix 2. These level tests focus on words from:

- The first 2,000 words.
- 3,000 word level.
- The AWL.
- 5,000 word level.
- 10,000 word level.

The 3,000, 5,000 and 10,000 levels are based on research carried out by Thorndike and Lorge.[4] Learners may think it is important to study words at these levels. However, these levels do not provide much return for learning effort and there are no real lists associated with them. Initially, it is better for learners to focus on high-frequency vocabulary (the first 2,000 words) and academic vocabulary (the AWL).

Nation[5] also has a productive test where students have to complete words missing in sentences to show that they can write the words correctly, know the correct words to use, and where they fit well in terms of meaning.

Once you find out roughly what vocabulary your learners may understand and can produce, what words they need to learn next, and what their purpose is for learning them, you need to establish what the learners need to know about the words.

What Aspects of a Word Do Learners Need to Know?

Many students focus on learning the translation of a word from their first language into the language they are learning and vice versa. The first language translation, however, is only one aspect of a word that learners need to know. There are many other aspects of a word that students need to know.[6] These include meaning, pronunciation, grammar, word families and words that commonly occur with (collocation[7]). Let's look at each of these aspects in turn.

Meaning

When we teach and learn a new word, we often focus first on the meaning. Meaning has a number of aspects to it such as the first-language meaning or translation. This book does not deal with first-language translation examples. Meaning can also include the word's meaning in a particular context. See Chapter 6 for suggestions on how to deal with the meanings of words in context.

Another aspect of meaning is the main or core meaning of the word.[8] You can look for a word's core meaning by looking for similarities in meanings of a word rather than focussing on any differences. It is worth looking at this concept of meaning as it is a good way to encourage learners to think deeply about a word's meaning. See Chapter 7 for more on teaching the core meaning of a word.

In some instances, learners may recognise the form of the word but may not understand how to use it in their speaking and writing.[9] An example is the two forms of "goodbye" in some languages. The person who is leaving uses a different expression from the one who is staying. This is a new concept for an English speaker, for whom *goodbye* covers both the leave-taker and the person staying. For a Spanish speaker, *lend* and *borrow* are the same word, *prestar*.[10] Learning these two words in English to replace one concept in Spanish can cause confusion between these two opposites.

Pronunciation

Learning to say a word is an important aspect of word knowledge. Learners have to learn to say a word clearly using the correct sounds and the right word stress. They may need training to become accurate in picking out the word when it is spoken and in saying the word to overcome problems like difficult sounds or combinations of letters.[11]

Here are some suggestions for the pronunciation of academic words:

- Plan to include pronunciation work in vocabulary lessons. If you plan for pronunciation work, you are less likely to forget to focus on it in class.
- Have reference texts nearby to consult when you are planning and teaching.[12]
- Encourage learners to learn phonetic symbols to help them pronounce new words. Learning one or two symbols a day is a reasonable goal, as long as each day the symbols look and sound very different.[13]

- Give learners many opportunities to say the key words and ensure that feedback is readily available on their pronunciation.
- Ask learners what pronunciation they want to be corrected on and how they want to be corrected.
- Practice words in and out of context. Give learners sample sentences to say and practice in class. The sentences might come from class texts or you could make them up on the spot.
- Focus on sound and spelling regularities so that learners become aware of how words might sound depending on how they are spelled. There are also rules on word stress that may help take away some of the guesswork for learners.[14]

See Chapter 12 for more suggestions on pronunciation and speaking activities.

Grammar

Learners need to know the grammar of words so they can use them accurately in their writing and speaking and can understand the words when they read and listen. For example, it is important to know whether a word is a noun, a verb, an adjective or an adverb. If it is a noun, is it countable and therefore can it be made into a plural?

Here are several key ideas for developing and maintaining grammatical accuracy awareness:

- Help your learners become aware or *noticing* the grammar of target words in context. Noticing words is a little like what happens when you are starting the process of buying a car or painting a house. Suddenly you start seeing cars and house colors that you never noticed before. For learners, noticing words in texts means that their attention is drawn to the word while they are reading. For example, you might ask learners to find an academic word that occurs frequently in a passage and count the number of occurrences of the word family.[15]
- Practice using the target words in a controlled situation using substitution tables or fill-in-the-blank exercises. These activities can help learners gain control of the language pattern.
- Encourage learners to seek feedback on their attempts to use the word and to analyze the feedback to achieve accuracy.
- Support learners in trying to use the vocabulary regularly.

- Work on class-based vocabulary errors from writing and speaking activities.
- Encourage learners to monitor a particular form or forms in their own writing and speaking.
- Focus on giving specific feedback on vocabulary use in writing tasks.
- Develop individual checklists of common errors for learners to use in editing their own work.
- Ensure learners develop good dictionary skills. For more on vocabulary learning and dictionary skills, see Chapter 7.

You might also like to introduce learners to a wide range of reference materials such as grammatical reference books, on-line materials, and dictionaries so they know the resources available to help them work on particular language problems. Reference materials might also help learners develop more complexity and accuracy in their use of vocabulary.[16] You can model the use of dictionaries and reference materials in your class by making them the focus of vocabulary-based activities.

Word Families

A word family usually includes all the inflected words related to a core word. You will be familiar with verb groups in English, such as *secure, secures, secured, securing*. Normally we think about verb groups as a basic unit of a word family. You could add in a noun form (*security*), as well as an adjective (*secure*) and an adverb (*securely*).

There are two more aspects of word formation we need to add to this picture.

- **Prefixes** (parts of a word that go before the stem, such as *pre, un,* and *dis*).
- **Suffixes** (parts of a word that go after the stem, such as *-ment, -ation* and *-ise*).
- Knowledge of prefixes and suffixes can help learners to build up their word family knowledge, such as, *like, likes, liked, liking, unlike, likeable*. For more on word parts, see Chapter 5.

Some word families are quite large, for example *analyze* has a large number of word family members.[17] Other words have no family members, such as *furthermore* and *albeit*. Still others have a word family that is used for the verb and the noun, such as *bond* (noun) as in *a bond between two people* and *bond* (verb) as in *the glue bonded the two surfaces together*.

Here are some key points about word families:

- Some word family members are more frequent than others. At first, students need to know and be able to appropriately use the most frequent members of word families.
- Learners can supplement their knowledge of other members of the word families as they come across them in texts.
- Learners seem to develop their knowledge of word forms incrementally.[18] That is, they build up their knowledge slowly. The more words learners know, the more likely they will know the family word members. Learners with a high-level vocabulary will still not know some word family members, however.
- Some word family members are better known than others.[19] Learners tend to know the verb and noun forms above the adjective and adverbial forms.[20] For example, *analyze* and *analysis* would be known before *analytical* and *analytically*.

Collocations

Collocations are words that go together or are frequently used together.[21] An example of collocations for the word *issue* might be *raise*, as in *raise an issue* or *address*, as in *address an issue*. An easy way to look for collocations in a text is to first identify the grammar of the word you are working on and then look for words around it that connect grammatically with that word. For example, if it is a noun such as *environment*, look for an adjective before the noun that is describing it. You may find *dirty*, *clean*, *natural* or *school*. These words would be collocates of the word *environment*.

Not all words are collocates for other words. Some words are specifically used in connection with others. For example, we talk about some people having *a high income* but not *a tall income*. However, a person can be *a tall person* or *a big person* but we would not say someone is *a high person* if you are talking about their height.

Collocations are a complex but interesting area of study and learning. Research is being carried out to discover more about them. Collocations are important because they can help learners build up chunks of language, teach learners to look for patterns of use, and can provide scaffolding for new pieces of language.

Here are some suggestions for ways to develop awareness of collocations in class in connection with academic vocabulary:

- Practice finding collocations in texts and presenting them as part of the learning of particular words. You could practice looking for collocations for the underlined words in the passage that follows.

OBJECTIVES OF FINANCIAL INFORMATION

The United States has a highly developed exchange <u>economy</u>. In this kind of economy, most goods and services are exchanged for money or claims to money instead of being used or bartered by their producers. Most business is carried on through corporations, including many extremely large firms that buy, sell, and <u>obtain</u> financing in U.S. and world markets.[22]

For *economy*, you might have found *highly developed* and *exchange*. For *obtain* you might have found *financing*.

- Have students match words with common collocations. See Chapter 11 for more activities using collocations.
- Have learners write or speak on a topic that encourages the use of these items together.
- Use cloze exercises with collocates or key items removed so learners are using one word as a key to finding the common collocation.

Endnotes

1. A word family is all the words that are related to each other through form and meaning. For example the word family of *hypothesis* includes *hypotheses, hypothesise, hypothetical, hypothetically* etc.

2. Nation, P. 2001. *Learning vocabulary in another language.* Cambridge: Cambridge University Press.

3. Schmitt, N. 2001. *Vocabulary in language teaching.* Cambridge: Cambridge University Press.

4. Thorndike, E. L. and I. Lorge. 1944. *The teacher's word book of 30,000 words.* New York: Teachers College, Columbia University.

5. Nation, 2001.

6. For more on learning and teaching aspects of knowing a word, see Nation, P. 2001. *Learning vocabulary in another language.* Cambridge: Cambridge University Press. Also, Schmitt, N. 2001. *Vocabulary in language teaching.* Cambridge: Cambridge University Press.

7. For example, if we take the word *analyze,* there are a number of words that we use often with it, such as *analyze a situation* or *analyze a company's expenses.* These examples are from *The American Heritage English as a second language dictionary.* 1998. Boston: Houghton Mifflin.

8. Visser, A. 1989. Learning core meanings. *Guidelines 11*(2), 10–17.

9. See Nation, P. 2001. *Learning vocabulary in another language.* Cambridge: Cambridge University Press, especially page 47.

10. Thank you to John Bunting for this example.

11. See Murphy, J. 2004. Word-level stress in EAP oral communication. *Houghton-Mifflin ESL/ELT Academic Success Newsletter 2,* 1–3 for ideas on teaching word stress and academic vocabulary.

12. Try O'Connor, J. D. 1980. *Better English Pronunciation.* Cambridge: Cambridge University Press as a reference text.

13. See the pronunciation guide in the inside cover of *The American Heritage English as a second language dictionary.* 1998. Boston: Houghton Mifflin.

14. See Digby, C. & J. Myers. 1993. *Making sense of spelling and pronunciation.* Hemel Hempstead: Prentice-Hall for more on sounds and spelling in English.

15. I heard of this idea at a MANATESOL workshop at Massey University in Palmerston North, New Zealand.

16. For ideas on grammar and vocabulary see Swan, M. 1995. *Practical English usage.* Oxford: Oxford University Press, Thornbury, S. 1999. *How to teach grammar.* Harlow: Pearson Education, Wajnryb, R. (1990). *Grammar dictation.* Oxford: Oxford University Press.

17. Think of as many word family members as you can for the word *analyze* and then think which you would teach first, how and why.

18. Schmitt, N., & C. Zimmerman. 2002. Derivative word forms: what do learners know? *TESOL Quarterly 36*(2), 145–171. Especially page 162.

19. Schmitt, N., & C. Zimmerman. 2002.

20. Schmitt, N., & C. Zimmerman. 2002.

21. For more reading on collocations, see Nation, P. 2001. *Learning vocabulary in another language.* Cambridge: Cambridge University Press and Lewis, M. (Ed.). 2000. *Teaching collocation.* Hove: Language Teaching Publications.

22. Needles, B., Jr., M. Powers & S. Crosson. 2005. *Principles of accounting.* Boston: Houghton Mifflin.

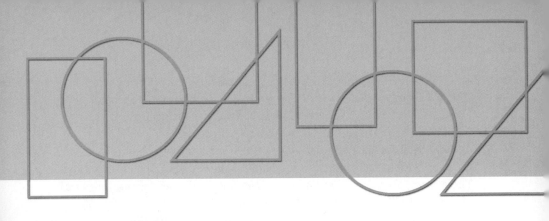

Principles of Learning Vocabulary

- What principles of learning vocabulary are important?
- How can we make these principles explicit to learners?

What Principles of Learning Vocabulary Are Important?

There are a number of principles behind learning and teaching vocabulary that should be kept in mind in any vocabulary programme. The principles we will look at in this section are frequency, repetition, spaced retrieval, the avoidance of interference and generation. In Part 3, we will look at how to build these principles into teaching and learning activities.

The Frequency Principle

In the introduction, we looked briefly at the principle of focussing on high-frequency items. The reason for this focus is that these words occur in many texts, spoken and written, and they form the building blocks of the language. The same principle applies in teaching words from the AWL.

My study showed that the first sublist of the AWL accounted for 3.5 percent of the words in a large body of written academic texts.[1] These words clearly occur often in the texts and are therefore worth spending time on learning and teaching.

As with any frequency-based list, the words in later sublists have lower frequencies than those in earlier lists. Because learners won't be meeting these lower-frequency AWL words as often, it is important that learners spend time both directly and indirectly on these words once the higher-frequency words are well established. See Chapter 3 for more on computer programmes and websites you can use to find out the frequency of words in texts.

The Repetition Principle

Repetition is a key part of learning words. It is difficult for words to stick in your memory if you see them only once. Also, as we saw in Chapter 1, there is more to knowing a word than just its direct translation from one language to another. Repetition allows learners to learn more about a word. It is important also because it helps learners build their knowledge of a word to the point of fluency.[2]

How many repetitions do learners need to learn a word and build fluency? The answer is not straightforward because there are so many aspects to learning a word and so many variables in the process. What we do know is that the more repetitions, the better.[3] In other words, if you spot opportunities for repetition of target academic words in class, then use them. Every little bit helps.

What are the key ideas to keep in mind with the repetition principle?

- Learners need to see the word in a wide range of contexts.
- Repetitions need to be spaced so that the learners have time for the word to sink in.[4] There should not be too long between repetitions or else the word will be forgotten—see the *principle of spaced retrieval* that follows.
- Encourage learners to notice words in the text so they don't miss the repetition. You can do this very simply by highlighting the word in some way and by paying attention to it in class.
- Make learners aware that they need repetitions both for developing comprehension in reading and listening, and for production in speaking and writing.

- Learners can reread materials for another exposure; also texts on similar topics may contain some of the same vocabulary.
- Reuse materials in different ways to ensure repetition. For example, a reading text can be made into a split information text, a dictation, a summary writing task or a note taking exercise.

The Principle of Spaced Retrieval

Have you observed learners looking up the same word in the dictionary twice within a short period of time? Why does that happen?

- Maybe the word is not important so learners don't make an effort to remember it.
- It could be too much time has gone by between repetitions, and learners forget the word.
- Perhaps the word is more likely to be remembered if it is needed often.

Lots of repetitions in the early stages of learning are important so that the chances of learners remembering the words will be higher. That is, there is not enough time to forget. This is the 'spaced' part of the principle of 'spaced retrieval'.[5]

Retrieval means that the learners recall the meaning or form of a word from their memory. Retrieval works on the idea that learners have to think deeply to find the meaning or the word in their memory. The process of thinking deeply and remembering strengthens a learner's knowledge of a word. The more often words are retrieved, the stronger the association or learning of the word becomes.[6]

One of the easiest ways of demonstrating retrieval for vocabulary learning is using flash cards. Flash cards have the target item on one side and the meaning on the other. Learners looking at one side of the card will not be able to see the other side and therefore, will have to retrieve the meaning or the word. They can then check the back to see if the information they retrieved is correct. Flash cards are a highly efficient way of learning vocabulary. See Chapter 5 on strategies for more discussion and suggestions using flash cards.

Other ways to build retrieval into vocabulary exercises include:

- Using word quizzes in class. For example, you give the meaning and the learners provide the word, or vice versa.
- Having a class vocabulary box. All new words from each day are put on cards and added to the box so learners can regularly review them.
- Developing cloze exercises or normal gap fills. Learners fill in words they are reviewing from the week.
- Talking to your students about spaced retrieval. Encourage them to build it into their own learning.

The Principle of Avoiding Interference

Have you learned or taught two words in another language that are opposites and then mixed up the words and their meanings? In my case, I learned these Hungarian words together:

meleg = hot
hideg = cold

You can perhaps understand why I ended up with this incorrect association:

meleg = cold*
hideg = hot*

To me, these words looked and sounded similar because they end with the same two letters. They also shared a meaning connected with temperature. It was summer so I decided to learn the word for *hot* first. Once I was comfortable with using that word, I moved on to learning the word for *cold*. I solved the confusion by concentrating on learning one of the words at a time, instead of trying to learn both.

Many teachers teach words in lexical sets, for example, teaching all the colours together or teaching opposites as part of a lesson. This approach can lead to more confusion than clarity.[7] So if the problem is that we tend to mix up words that look and sound the same, what can we do to ensure that learners avoid interference in their learning? Here are some suggestions:

- Avoid teaching two such items together. First teach the item used most frequently. Once that word is firmly established in the learner's vocabulary, it will be easier to focus on the second word.[8]

- Teach only the word that appears in the text. That is, if the text only uses the word *migrate*, then avoid the temptation of teaching *immigrate* and *emigrate* at the same time.
- Make sure that similar looking words do not occur in the same text or if they do, make learners aware of the cause of interference. In this way, teachers and learners are both working to reduce the chances of confusion.
- Make sure learners avoid trying to learn from lists and dictionaries by starting with words that begin with *a* and then moving on to words that begins with *b*.

The problem with this method can be illustrated using several words from my Academic Word List.[9] Here is a selection of AWL words starting with *con*:

| concept | conclude | concurrent | conduct | confer |
| confine | confirm | conflict | conform | consent |

There are two key points to make about this list.

1. These words all look similar. They all start with *con*. Although the ends of the words look different, the beginnings are too similar. Learning from lists going from A through Z is counterproductive to learning.
2. It is better to focus on the most frequent words first. Once these words have been firmly established, learners can then work on the next most frequent words. Working on words as they occur in context and using the lists as a reference point can counteract some of the negative effects of learning a list alphabetically. [10]

Try this ranking exercise yourself. Use your intuition to rank the *con* words listed in order of frequency. Check your guesses against the AWL in Appendix 1. Find the sublist they are in and therefore which words are more frequent than the others in academic texts. Did your intuition prove you right?

The Generation Principle

Generation means that learners use or encounter a word in a new way from how they met the word before.[11] The effort involved in speaking and writing a word has positive effects on learning. Also, meeting known words in new contexts while reading and listening increases a learner's knowledge about the word.[12] How can we encourage generation in our academic vocabulary activities?

- Ensure that your language learning programme has a wide range of reading and listening materials so learners can encounter the target vocabulary in new contexts. For more on academic vocabulary and reading, see Chapters 8 and 9. For academic vocabulary and listening, see Chapters 10 and 11.
- Provide plenty of speaking and writing activities that use the target words as part of their focus. For more on academic vocabulary and speaking, see Chapters 12 and 13. For academic vocabulary and writing, see Chapters 14 and 15.

In Part 3, we will be looking at how to build generation into academic vocabulary learning tasks in more detail.

How Can We Make These Vocabulary Learning Principles Explicit to Learners?

- Set aside time in your class to discuss key concepts of vocabulary learning such as frequency, aspects of knowing a word, collocations, and interference.
- Have each student rank the four principles of frequency, repetition, spaced retrieval, and generation into a personal order of importance and then explain to each other the reasons behind the ranking.
- Have the class prepare a short talk or poster on principles of vocabulary learning with examples of how they approach their own learning to illustrate their points.
- Relate classroom vocabulary tasks to the aspects of learning a word and principles.
- Have students evaluate methods of learning vocabulary or keeping records by applying the principles from this chapter. For example, you could examine using flash cards for learning vocabulary and see how repetition, spaced retrieval and generation are built into this learning strategy. See Chapter 5 for more on this using flash cards.

The principles in this chapter are very important to learning and teaching words. Throughout this book we will return to them again and again.

Endnotes

1. Coxhead, A. 2000. A new academic word list. *TESOL Quarterly, 34,*(2) 213–238.

2. Nation, P. 2001. *Learning vocabulary in another language.* Cambridge: Cambridge University. See especially pages 74 and 75.

3. For a discussion on repetition and its effect on learning in detail, see Nation, P. 2001. *Learning vocabulary in another language.* Cambridge: Cambridge University Press.

4. Baddeley, A. 1990. *Human memory.* London: Lawrence Erlbaum Associates.

5. For a wide-ranging discussion on spaced retrieval, see Nation, P. 2001. *Learning vocabulary in another language.* Cambridge: Cambridge University Press.

6. Baddeley, 1990.

7. For more on how to avoid interference in learning and teaching words, see Nation, P. 2000. Learning vocabulary in lexical sets: dangers and guidelines. *TESOL Journal, 9* (2), 6–10.

8. Nation, 2001.

9. You can find the Academic Word List sublists in Appendix 1. Also, check the websites listed on the website for this book at http://www.college.hmco.com/esl/instructors

10. For more on how to avoid interference in learning and teaching word, see Nation, P. 2000. Learning vocabulary in lexical sets: dangers and guidelines. *TESOL Journal, 9* (2), 6–10.

11. Nation, 2001. See pages 68–72 for an in-depth discussion on generation.

12. See Wittrock, M., C. Marks, & M. Doctorow (1975). Reading as a generative process. *Journal of Educational Psychology 11,* 87–95.

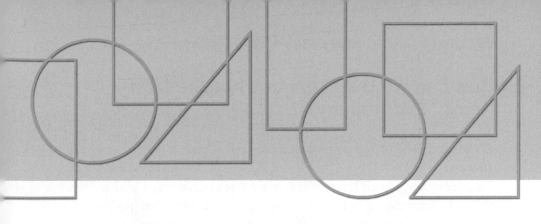

Chapter 3

Acquiring New Items of Vocabulary

FEATURED IN THIS CHAPTER

- How can we help learners acquire new items of vocabulary?
- How can you find out the frequency of academic words in a passage?

How do we learn new words? Young children acquire new words[1] in their first language every day at an amazing rate. Some estimate that children learn up to three new words a day[2] and that by the time they are in their late teens, they already have almost 20,000 words in their vocabulary. In comparison, the average second-language learner who has been studying a language for several hours a week may know between 3,000–5,000 words. The difference between 20,000 and 3,000–5,000 words is enormous. Learners need to fill this gap, especially if they are learning vocabulary for academic purposes. How can teachers help learners acquire academic vocabulary?

How Can We Help Learners Acquire New Items of Vocabulary?

Acquiring new words is a complex process. Research so far has not told us all we need to know about how it is done. We do know that there are a number of key principles involved, as we saw in Chapters 1 and 2. Also, there are many aspects of word knowledge, as we discussed in Chapter 1. Furthermore, I know from my own experience in language learning and teaching that sometimes a word just won't stick. It is important to remember that fully acquiring items of vocabulary is a process that takes time. Vocabulary knowledge is incremental in nature.[3]

We can help facilitate acquiring new academic words or building knowledge of partially acquired vocabulary by developing a range of activities and using different approaches in class. These should encourage learners to notice, gain control of, and develop fluency in using the words. Learners may start by finding a word they recognize but don't know its meaning as it is used in the text. Or perhaps they encounter a word they don't know at all and will have to build up their knowledge from the beginning. Acquiring new words is a complex process and no learners will be at the same point at the same time with the same word.[4]

In this chapter, I aim to give you some practical ideas to help with each part of the process. For activities to put these ideas into practice, see the chapters on each individual skill area. Where you and your learners start will depend on their prior knowledge and needs for the words you are focussing on. Is there an end to the process of acquiring new words? Probably not, because as they say, if you don't use it, you lose it!

One final point is that learners need to be actively involved in the process of acquiring new words. They also need to understand that the way they approach learning new words can affect their learning. In other words, learners need to know how and why they are learning these words.

Finding a Word in a Text

One of the first steps in helping learners become aware of a word is to find it in a text. To help your students expand their academic vocabulary, you should look for words that have these characteristics:

- The words seem important in understanding the key ideas in the text.
- Their frequency in academic English is high.
- They represent a gap in the students' language knowledge.

You can use a reading in their textbook or other material that is appropriate for their level and interest. It is important to work from a text rather than a list of words because:

- The words will appear in context.
- The learners will find out more about the word through being exposed to it with its common collocations, grammatical form and word family members.
- This method avoids the risk of learners becoming confused because they are trying to learn similar-looking words together.
- Learners will have a model of how the words occur naturally in a text.
- The context may provide meaning for the words.

Noticing the Target Language

We need to help students notice the pattern of the target words in the context of the message in the text. It is also important for them to realise how knowledge of the language pattern is affecting their understanding. That is, if there is a gap in their vocabulary knowledge, they will not get meaning from the text.

How can you foster noticing language when students are focused on the meaning?

- Use comprehension questions that focus on the target words.
- Ask concept-checking questions that encourage the learners to evaluate whether they have understood the text.

Paying Attention to the Form of the Target Words

By isolating the pattern and looking closely at the details of the target words, you can help learners pay attention to the form of words. You can do this by asking students to tell you what follows or is before the word in the sentence. For example, you can ask them to:

- Put the target word on the board by itself for everyone to look at closely.
- Notice the grammatical pattern of the target words in their contexts.
- Notice the spelling of the words.
- Find collocations for the target words.

Repeated Processing

Repeated processing involves looking back at the target language in its context to check that learners have understood the message. They can also look for other occurrences of the same target language in other contexts in the same text, or in other segments of communication. You can ask the learners to:

- Look at the target words again in their original context.
- Search the text for more examples of the target words.
- Explore how the target language could be used in other situations.

Practice to Gain Control of the Target Language

Practicing the target language in a controlled situation is important because it helps learners gain control over their use of the words.[5] They can do this by:

- using substitution tables;
- supplying forms in fill-in-the-blank exercises. See Chapter 13 for an example;
- filling in crosswords;
- matching words and meanings;
- playing word games with the target words. These could be card games where learners match words with, for example, their synonyms (words that mean the same), common academic collocates, word family members or antonyms (opposites);
- answering multiple-choice meaning-based questions and answers;

- completing decision-making tasks such as ranking or selecting activities where the target words are central to completing the tasks.

Always test out your exercise on colleagues or by completing it yourself so you know it works well before you hand it out to students.

See Chapter 2 for an exercise on finding collocations in passages.

Recycling the Target Language

Recycling vocabulary involves using the target vocabulary in speaking and writing, within a familiar context. This part of the processes is recycling. Learners are working with the words to gain mastery of them. Activities that encourage recycling include:

- retelling the text either by speaking or writing. You can find examples of this exercise in the Oral Communication books in this series.
- employing the 4-3-2 speaking fluency activity whereby learners use the target words in a short talk and deliver it to a different listener for 4 minutes, then 3, and finally 2 minutes;[6]
- having learners make comprehension tasks with the target words for each other;
- having learners speak on the topic of the text while trying consciously to use the new items. See Chapter 13 for examples of speaking activities using academic vocabulary.

Seeking and Analyzing Feedback on Attempts to Use the Language

Learners need to seek and analyze feedback on their attempts to use the target language. The purpose is to achieve accuracy. They can get the feedback from a variety of sources other than you including:

- other learners in the class or the school;
- other speakers of the target language in the community;
- dictionaries;
- reference books;
- original source materials used in class.

Teachers and learners need to create opportunities for practice and feedback. Meeting a word once will never be enough to learn it. Producing a word once also will never be enough to ensure that a learner can produce it accurately from then on. Learners need opportunities to practice and get feedback so that they can start to remember words on a daily, weekly and monthly basis. See Chapter 12 for more on giving feedback on vocabulary in student speaking and Chapter 15 for feedback on vocabulary in student writing.

Maintaining the Target Language

The final step is that learners need to **maintain the target language** in their language use by:

- noticing it in texts;
- using it regularly and working on accuracy. Testing out new words usually involves making errors and teachers need to be ready to help develop accuracy through some form of correction and feedback;
- attending to feedback that they get on their use of the target language in their speaking and writing.

How Can You Find Out the Frequency of Academic Words in a Passage?

After you select a text to use with your students, you can analyze the vocabulary using the AWL Highlighter—a website created by Sandra Haywood.[7] The AWL Highlighter highlights the AWL words in text that you cut and paste into the website so you can easily see which words come from the list. Here is a sample of text from an earlier chapter with all the AWL words from all the sublists highlighted:

> **TEXT WITH AWL WORDS HIGHLIGHTED FROM SUBLISTS 1–10.**
>
> The **principles** of frequency, repetition and spaced retrieval from **Chapters** 1 and 2 are clearly **represented** in this **process**. This is because they are key to the **process** of words becoming part of what we call our 'mental lexicon' or our own **internal** dictionaries. Another important point is that learners need to be actively **involved** in this **process** and to understand each part. In other words, learners need to know how and why they are learning these words.

In addition to checking the particular texts, you can find out about the general frequency of words in the text by using the Web Vocabulary Profiler,[8] developed by Tom Cobb or the Frequency Level Checker, developed by Joyce Maeda.[9] Using these programmes you can mark up a text according to whether the words occur in the first or second 1,000 words of the General Service List (West, 1953), or the Academic Word List (Coxhead, 2000), or whether they do not occur in any of these lists. Look also at the British National Corpus website[10] for more up-to-date word frequency information.

Endnotes

1. Remember that how you count a word can change the total amount of words people know very quickly. Do we count a word as one word on its own, or do we count the whole word family as one word?
2. Goulden, R., P. Nation, & Read, J. 1990. How large can a receptive vocabulary be? *Applied Linguistics 11*, 341–363.
3. Schmitt, N. 2000. *Vocabulary in language teaching*. Cambridge: Cambridge University Press. See especially page 117.
4. See Ellis, N. 1995. Vocabulary acquisition: Psychological perspectives and pedagogical implications. *The Language Teacher*, 19(2), 12–16 for an interesting discussion on the acquisition of new words.
5. See the activity chapters for each individual skill in Part Three of this book and the website for this book at http://www.college.hmco.com/esl/students for examples and more.
6. Maurice, K. 1983. The fluency workshop. *TESOL Newsletter, 8*, 83.
7. The AWL Highlighter by Sandra Haywood, available at http://www.nottingham.ac.uk/~alzsh3/acvocab/awlhighlighter.htm
8. The Web Vocabulary Profiler, available at http://www.lextutor.ca/vp/eng/, was developed by Tom Cobb and can work with English and French.
9. The Frequency Level Checker, available at http://language.tiu.ac.jp/flc/, was developed by Joyce Maeda.
10. The British National Corpus frequency lists based largely on an academic body of texts are available at http://www.natcorp.ox.ac.uk/. For more on the British National Corpus word counts, see Leech, G., Rayson, P., & Wilson, A. (2001). *Word frequencies in written and spoken English*. Harlow Essex: Longman.

Chapter **4**

Teaching Academic Vocabulary

FEATURED IN THIS CHAPTER

- What is rich instruction in relation to vocabulary learning?
- How can we fit academic vocabulary instruction into language programs?
- How can we clearly explain the meanings of academic words?

The teaching and learning of academic vocabulary has to be carefully planned. Teachers and learners need to take full advantage of precious learning time in and out of class. Planning is also required for explaining academic words to good effect.

What Is *Rich Instruction*[1] in Relation to Vocabulary Learning?

Rich instruction in classrooms basically means supporting our learners as much as we can in their vocabulary learning. In practical terms, rich instruction means thinking about whether your classroom time includes these elements:

- Goals for individual students that focus on learning academic vocabulary;
- Understanding which words learners should focus on depending on their needs;
- Clear explanations that are supported if possible by pictures and examples;
- Many exposures to the words;
- Opportunities to use the words when speaking and writing and to gain feedback;
- Skills in strategy use for vocabulary learning.

By prioritizing vocabulary learning and teaching in the classroom and by applying the ideas of rich instruction, we are making a conscious effort to develop our learners' skills and knowledge in this area. How can we make sure that this commitment is reflected in the overall program of study at college level?

How Can We Fit Academic Vocabulary Instruction into Language Programs?

The Four Strands of a Language Program[2]

Nation outlines four strands in a language program.

1. **Meaning-focussed input** is when learners are listening or reading and gaining exposure to new language. They are focussed on the meaning of what they are hearing or reading.
2. **Meaning-focussed output** is when learners are writing or speaking and focussing on the message they are trying to convey.

3. **Form-focussed instruction** is when there is direct teaching and learning of vocabulary, including pronunciation, spelling and grammar of target words.
4. **Fluency** is when the learners are speaking and writing and building fluency in using words they already know.

Nation[3] recommends having a balance of these four strands in any language instruction program. This model of four strands can help teachers analyze how their classroom activities fit into the overall language program.

Here is a checklist of questions to help you think about how academic vocabulary fits into your program.

- Have you thought about the processes responsible for how vocabulary is acquired (talked about in Chapter 3), and how vocabulary-based activities fit into the acquisition process? For example, where does an activity that learners match words with their meanings fit? Where does an activity whereby learners are writing an academic argument on a new topic fit?
- Have you devoted some time to talking about and exploring the processes of language acquisition we have outlined? For example, talk with your learners about the importance of noticing words and its effect on their language learning.
- Have you made the goal of each vocabulary activity clear to learners?
- Have you checked that words introduced into the program are repeatedly focussed on in a variety of ways in subsequent classes?
- Have you built rich instruction into your program? Are learners meeting and using words in a variety of ways that encourage them to explore and use the language?
- Have you discussed the principles of learning vocabulary, from Chapter 2, with your class? Just to remind you, they are:
  - Learn and teach high-frequency vocabulary first.
  - Remember to repeat exposures to words.
  - Include spaced retrieval in learning and teaching.
  - Try to avoid interference between words that sound or look similar or are opposites.
- Have you included direct learning strategies such as flash cards and the key word technique in your program? See Chapter 5 for more details and examples of direct learning strategies.
- Have you included indirect learning strategies such as extensive reading in your program? See Chapter 6 for more details and examples of indirect learning strategies.

- Have you focussed the class tasks or activities on academic vocabulary?
- Have you made sure that the tasks you have designed have an academic focus? For example, are your students reading academic texts? If they are reading fiction, they will get exposure to high frequency words but very few academic words.[4]
- Have you activated prior knowledge about the key words and integrated it into the vocabulary learning activities?
- Have you set aside time dedicated to vocabulary learning?
- Have you decided how and when you will test the vocabulary?

How Can We Clearly Explain the Meanings of Academic Words?

Once you decide on how vocabulary fits into your program of study, you need to think about how you will explain the words to learners. Some words are very easy to explain. *Banana*, for example, is a word that requires almost no introduction. Other words are very high frequency, so learners have many chances to meet them again and again or they may have already met them before they come up in a lesson. In most beginner classes I have taught, learners had already acquired words like *hello* and the phrase *thank you* before they even stepped foot into my class.

Academic words, unlike some high-frequency words like *banana*, can be difficult to explain. For example, how would you teach the words *paradigm*, *mediate* and *underlie*?

Here are some reasons why academic words can cause difficulties when we try to explain them to students:

- Academic words tend to be connected to abstract ideas rather than concrete ones. Compare, for example, teaching *banana* (a high-frequency word) to teaching *phenomenon* (an academic word).
- Over 80 percent of the words in the AWL come from Latin or Greek.[5] Some first-language learners will therefore have more problems with academic vocabulary than others. For example, a learner with Russian as a first language will have more academic words in common with English than a learner with Chinese as a first language. This is because Russian has more words from Latin and Greek than Chinese has.

- Academic words can be very long, for example, *facilitation* has five syllables. This might be why some learners find academic words hard to recall and pronounce.
- Sometimes academic words look a lot like each other. Compare *contrary, contrast, contradict* and *contract*. These words can be easily confused because they all start with the same letters (*contra*) and sound similar.

Here are some key ideas to keep in mind when deciding how to introduce the meaning of a word.

- Give easy to understand and preferably short explanations.[6] For example, if someone asks you what *data* is, you could say it is *information*, or you could tell them it is *information gathered through research or an empirical study*. Think about what is most important for learners to come away with from their first encounters with the words.
- Plan how you will explain the meaning of words before you step into the classroom. Many academic words are abstract, so finding pictures to illustrate them may not be easy. You may be able to use phrases to help. For example, you could teach *an abstract idea* instead of just teaching that the word *abstract* is an adjective.
- Use techniques such as breaking academic words into word parts because it may make the words easier to understand and learn.[7] For example *unpredictable* can be broken down like this—*un* = not/*pre* = before/*dict* = say/*able* = can or able to.
- Think about how to explain a word's core or underlying meaning.[8] Generally, the various common uses of a word share a core or central meaning. For example, *extract* can be used in several contexts. You can:
  - *Extract a tooth* at the dentist.
  - *Extract money* from a money machine.
  - *Extract meaning* from a text.
  - *Extract oil* from the ground.

Based on these examples, what is the core meaning of *extract*? Can you think of an action you could use to demonstrate *extract* while you are giving these examples? See Chapter 7 for more examples of how to introduce and exploit the learning of a word's core meaning.

- Build on your students' background knowledge. You can help learners with new words by using explanations that directly relate to them in some way. Here are two examples of the same activity. The one on the left uses easier ideas for learners to use to discuss the word *crucial*. The list on the right has more academic input (words from the AWL are in **bold**).

The word *crucial* is an academic word meaning *very important*. Which three items in the lists do you believe to be *crucial* for your lives and why?	
Air	A clean **environment**
Water	A stable **economy**
Computers	**Innovative technology**
Friends	A strong family **focus**
Music	A loving **partnership**
Television	**Physical** health
Anything else?	Anything else?

- Try to engage the attention of learners so they are actively working to understand the meaning of the words. You can use activities that encourage the learners to make guesses about the meanings and to discuss them with each other. You could ask learners to teach each other target words. This is a real way of getting learners involved!
- Use examples from passages where a word's meaning is given by a definition, a synonym, or an example. For example, *an innovation, or new development, can be very exciting.* A word might also be defined as being the opposite to another word the students know already. For example, *a modern, as opposed to traditional, approach could be taken.*
- Check regularly that students have retained the words. There are many ways to check vocabulary comprehension and retention. Here are some basic ideas:
  - Conducting simple ask and answer sessions where the class supplies the meaning of a word you give them or supplies the word if you give a meaning. Quizzes and class competitions like this work well.
  - Using concept-checking questions such as "Does X mean Y or Z?" and "What's another word for X?" to stimulate retrieval of target words and meanings.

- Matching card activities with meanings and words work well.
- Having learners test each other on words, meanings, spelling, collocations, etc., can be encouraging and motivating.
- Spelling bees on target words can be fun.
- Using the target words in games such as Pictionary and Hangman as whole-class or group activities can encourage learners to retrieve the spelling of words and help them with typical English word patterns.

Think about the time you have available for explaining words. Consider carefully how many words learners can usefully deal with in a class. You will need to consider their proficiency level, how difficult the words are, what background knowledge the learners have, and what the learners need to do with the words.[9] One of the reasons why the AWL was broken into 10 sublists is that lists of 60 words are more usable during a short course of study than trying to cover the whole 570 words at once.

Endnotes

1. For more on rich instruction, see Nation, P. 2001. *Learning vocabulary in another language*. Cambridge: Cambridge University Press.
2. Nation, P. 2001. *Learning vocabulary in another language*. Cambridge: Cambridge University Press.
3. Nation, 2001. See especially page 390 for a summary of the four strands and activities that fit each strand.
4. Coxhead, A. 2000. A new academic word list. *TESOL Quarterly, 34*(2), 213–238.
5. Coxhead, 2000.
6. Nation, 2001. See Chapter 3 book for more on teaching and explaining vocabulary.
7. Nation, 2001. See especially page 21.
8. Nation, 2001.
9. Thornbury, S. 2002. *How to teach vocabulary*. Longman: Harlow, Essex. See especially pages 75 and 76.

Part **2**

Strategies for Learning Vocabulary

Chapter **5**

Direct Learning Strategies

FEATURED IN THIS CHAPTER

- What are direct learning strategies?
- How can students learn academic vocabulary using flash cards?
- What is the key-word technique?
- How can learning word parts help with learning academic vocabulary?

Strategies are techniques or methods used for learning vocabulary. They include ways to learn words, to understand them in texts, and to maintain them in your learners' memories. These strategies need to be taught, regularly reviewed or used in class in order for them to become a normal part of a language learning routine. Lessons can be planned around teaching or revising strategies.

What Are Direct Learning Strategies?

One main idea behind deliberate or direct learning is that learners spend their time specifically on learning the word.[1] They can do this in many ways. In this section we will look at several ways that learners can focus directly on learning words. There is plenty of research evidence that such learning is very effective and is an important component of a well-balanced learning program.[2] I like teaching learners about using flash cards, the key-word technique and word parts because they are practical ideas that any learner can use or adapt.

How Can Students Learn Academic Vocabulary Using Flash Cards?

A flash card is a piece of cardboard or stiff paper about three-by-five-inches. The new word is written on one side. Your learners might want to add more information on this side, such as:

- pronunciation;
- part of speech;
- word stress.

The other side has the meaning of the word (in English or the learners' first language—this is something your learners need to decide). They might also add in:

- a sample collocation;
- a sentence to show the word or phrase in context;
- word family members.

Learners can work on flash cards alone or as a class. They can have their own pile of cards with words they need to focus on, keeping them in their pockets for reviewing at odd times during the day. About 20 words a week is a good number for a learner to work on. They can retrieve these aspects of a word using flash cards:

- meaning—in their first language or in English;
- spelling;
- collocations;
- pronunciation;
- word family members.

Learners can also try to put together sentences in their own words and the words on the cards.

Your class could also keep a vocabulary box. Learners can make up flash cards based on the day's class and keep the words in the box for review at any time. A vocabulary box is one way to reinforce the connection between vocabulary and other class work. It also supports learners with their use of the technique and reinforces it as a useful way to learn words in another language.

Why Are Flash Cards and Vocabulary Boxes Effective?

- Learners are responsible for the information on the cards, so they are highly aware that others are basing their learning on the accuracy of their flash cards.
- The cards are a reliable source for self-study and the students know precisely why each card is in the box and are able to evaluate which word to focus on.
- The students know where the words came from and they can refer back to the original source.
- Flash cards are easy to handle.
- Flash cards ensure that learners cannot see words or expressions and their meanings at the same time. This provides opportunity for recall or retrieval to take place.
- More than one student can work with the cards at any one time.
- The cards can be shuffled to avoid learning one word after the other or in alphabetical order.
- The cards can be used for intensive study in and out of class.

Some of the expressions and words in the box for an English for Academic Purposes class I taught at Victoria University in New Zealand included these words: *intense, interior, reveal, so-called, perspective, recombine, capability, interference, apparently, adjust,* and something *differs from* something else.

Using Flash Cards

There are many activities for flash cards in classes. The following is a selection based on recognition of words or receptive learning.

- **Spelling**—*How do you spell XXXX?*
- **Word families**—*X is the noun, what is the verb/adjective etc.?*

- **Collocation**—*What is a common collocation for the word XXXX?*
- **Meaning**—*This is the meaning, what is the word,* or *this is the word, what is the meaning, or XXXX means XXXX, is that right? (If not, what does it mean?)*
- **Production**—*Can you make a sentence with the word XXXX?*

- Have learners test each other in pairs or groups. They swap cards when they finish and form another pair or group. This ensures that learners work with a variety of words each time.
- Test the class using the questions above. As a follow-up activity, students can check their answers in pairs or as a group and then write the answers on the board. A quick post-test question and answer session can also draw attention to words and meanings that learners may have had difficulty with during the exercise.
- Have learners rank or group words into different categories. For example, learners can group the cards according to:
  - a topic;
  - similar connotations or another kind of connection;
  - same stress patterns;
  - opposites;
  - similar meanings;
  - similar spelling or word family patterns.
- Use the cards as the basis for dictations.
- Read or play a text and have learners order the words as they hear them in the text.
- Create fill-in-the-blank exercises using words from the cards. Have learners select cards and a topic to write about. Then, in pairs, they write their text, leaving gaps for other students to fill in the words or expressions from the cards. The original pairs correct the exercises completed by other students.
- Have learners create comprehension tasks such as true/false or multi-choice, making sure items from the cards are a key part of the task.
- Create error correction or form-focussed exercises based on errors made by students in writing and speaking the words from the box.
- Create computer crosswords. The clues could be common collocates, meanings, word family members or synonyms.[3]
- Have learners mark the stress on words.[4]

What Is the Key-Word Technique?

The key-word technique is another way to directly learn words. Using this strategy, learners develop a mental picture combining the meaning and sound of a word in the second language with the meaning and sound of a word in their first language.[5] This process involves deep thinking about the meaning and sound of a word, and this can lead to strong learning and remembering. The following example of the key-word technique from my own learning comes from Hungarian:

Target word and meaning: labda = ball

Here is my connection with the key-word technique for this word:

> **lab** sounds like *lob* meaning *to throw something a short distance*
> **da** is the short form of the word **Dad**.

I connect the meanings and sounds in English and Hungarian and my mental picture for this word is *lobbing or throwing a ball to my father*. The more imaginative the picture, the more memorable it is so maybe picture the ball as a big, bright beach ball.

Here are some key points to remember about the key-word technique.

- Learners sometimes struggle to find words with similar sounds in their first language. They might need, for example, to just focus on the initial letter or the middle of the word. They may need to stretch reality a little to make a connection. The more way out the connection is, the better.
- Learners may not find describing mental pictures easy. You could try to get them to draw a picture if they have difficulty describing the connection they have made.
- Start learners off with easier, less abstract vocabulary before working with more complex academic words.
- If you have a class with mostly the same first language and you share that language, then you are at an advantage for helping learners find meaning and sound "hooks" into this technique.
- If you have a mixed class you can possibly use connections with other words in English instead of first language examples. An example is:

    > *coincide* sounds a little like *go inside*
    > image = a whole class trying to enter an office door together as their individual visits *coincide*.

The key-word technique needs a lot of practice. Give your learners plenty of examples and spread the time over a couple of lessons so they can get comfortable using the technique. You could try to build the key-word technique into lessons with quick questions to guide the learners into thinking about words using it. Remember also that while this method may not suit everyone's learning style, it can be highly effective.[6]

How Can Learning Word Parts Help Vocabulary Learning?

Many longer and academic English words can be broken into word parts. Affixes are the parts that are added to word stems. Prefixes, such as *un* meaning *not*, are added to the front of word stems. Suffixes, such as *-able* or *-ility* are added to the ends of word stems. Apart from their positions on the word stems, there is another key difference between prefixes and suffixes. This difference is:

- Prefixes usually change the meaning of a word. For example, *happy* with the prefix *un-* becomes *unhappy*, *possible* with the prefix *im-* becomes *impossible*.
- Suffixes change the grammar or form of the word. For example, *communicate* (the verb) with the suffix *-ation* becomes *communication* (the noun), *care* (noun) with the suffix *-ful* becomes *careful* (adjective).

It is also important to know that prefixes can be **free** or **bound**.

- **Free forms** make up words that, without the prefix, can stand alone. An example of this would be *antisocial*. If you take away *anti*, the word *social* remains.
- **Bound forms** are words whose letters without the prefix do not make a word. An example of this is *communicate*. Take away the prefix *com* meaning *with* or *together* and the remaining part *unicate* does not stand on its own.

Free forms are easier to pull apart and analyze than bound forms because free forms operate with recognizable words.

Why Should Learners Learn About Common Affixes?

- Learning the meaning of common prefixes can help learners guess what a word might mean.
- Learning the forms of common affixes can help learners guess the grammar of a word. An example of this is *organise,* a verb that becomes a noun, *organization* when the ending *-ation* is attached. Another example is the adverbial suffix *ly* usually added to adjectives to make adverbs, as in *quick—quickly.* When guessing meaning from context, learners may be able to use word parts to help them successfully guess the meaning of the unknown word.
- Word family formations rely on affixes.

Examples of Prefix and Suffix Tasks for the Classroom

Here is an example of a classroom task[7] involving a list of common English prefixes with examples of AWL words. Learners A and B have the same worksheet but are missing different information on some common prefixes. Learner A's worksheet would look like this:

Prefixes Worksheet for Learner A[8]			
Prefix	**Meaning**	**Example word**	**Other forms**
ab-	from, away	abstract	a-, abs-
anti-	against		
com-		communicate	co-, col-, con-, cor-

Students work in pairs exchanging information on their pages through listening and speaking, making sure they carefully complete their worksheets. They can then use the worksheet as a study guide, for testing each other on the form, meaning and examples of each prefix, or for self-testing by covering up one section of the paper.

Learners should learn and test the prefixes randomly to avoid interference between prefixes that look similar. The principle of avoiding interference outlined in Chapter 2 works for any kind of word learning, including prefixes.

You could focus on 10 common prefixes, their meanings and forms every week. You could help learners notice common prefixes in class texts or vocabulary exercises. Regular reviews are important also. You could also help learners notice the prefixes in words in their reading texts.

Other word-part activities include:

- Having learners test each other using a table like the one given.
- Breaking up individual words as they encounter them in class.
- Quizzing learners on how many words starting with the same prefix they can list.
- Playing memory games that have groups of learners reassembling words from cards showing word parts.
- Using crosswords based around prefixes.[9]
- Having regular slots for class key words with multi-choice prefix items. For example, the prefix for the word meaning 'not logical' is:

  1. il-
  2. im-
  3. un-
  4. mis-

Often working a little bit with affixes is more effective than just one lesson.[10] Here is a sample activity with prefixes.[11]

Prefixes Worksheet

There is some information missing in the following table. Complete the words using your knowledge of English prefixes.

PREFIX	MEANING	EXAMPLE WORD
dis-		
	former	
mis-		

Suffix Activities

Here are some sample suffix activities focussed on learners recognising the suffixes, their part of speech (for example, noun, verb, adjective, adverb) and giving examples of words with the same patterns. They range in difficulty from all or most of the information supplied in some way, to learners needing to supply information and examples from their own knowledge.

The exercises that follow are designed to help learners recognise the most common English suffixes and to provide practice in their use to change a word's grammar so it fits properly into a sentence. Research shows that learners tend to know mostly the verb and noun forms of words in a word family.[12] You can download fuller versions of these charts from the website for this book.

Suffixes

Complete the table with the part of speech, suffix and example words. Add one more word that uses the same suffix. Be ready to discuss your answers.

Part of speech	Suffix	Example	Your example
adverb	-ly		
		partnership	
		communicate	

Suffixes: Word Families

Complete the following word families.

NOUN	ADJECTIVE	VERB
communication		
		manipulate
acknowledgement		
economy		

Suffixes Worksheet

Suffix	Part of speech	Example word	Other example words and notes
-ise/-ize	*Verb*	*theorise*	
-tion			
		communicate	
-ify			

Other Suffix Activities

- Having learners fill-in-the-blanks after changing the prefix or suffix to complete a meaningful sentence.
- Using a list of suffixes, such as the ones in the worksheet, to self-test. Have learners cover the part of speech, look at the suffix and recall its part of speech. Next have them cover the examples and recall them by looking at the suffix and part of speech.
- Encouraging learners to do independent study by keeping a vocabulary list of words they find during the week that have regular suffixes.
- Having learners check on-line sources for other suffixes and exercises with affixes.
- Encouraging learners to notice suffixes when they are reading. In particular they could focus on new word-family members and changes in spelling of unfamiliar words.

The Root Stems of Words

Some teachers draw their learners' attention to the stems of words. For example, *vis* meaning *see* can be helpful to know when it comes to these words: *visible, visual, invisible, invisibility* etc. Sometimes this is a very fruitful activity because the root is common and easy to see. For example, *form* is part of *deform* and *reform*, *spect* is part of *inspect* and *spectacles*.[13] Be careful with stems because some are extremely rare and not worth the effort of learning. Other stems can be difficult to see and frustrating to learners.

Endnotes

1. Nation, P. 2001. *Learning vocabulary in another language.* Cambridge: Cambridge University Press.
2. Nation, 2001. See especially 296–303.
3. The website for this book has a link to another website with crossword puzzles. Go to http://www.college.hmco.com/esl/students for that link.
4. You can find more ideas and examples of academic vocabulary, word stress and syllables in the Oral Communication books in this Houghton Mifflin series and in John Murphy's book in this same series called *Essentials of teaching academic oral communication.*
5. For more on the key-word technique, see Nation, 2001, especially pages 311–314.
6. For a more in-depth discussion and research on the key-word technique, see Nation, 2001.
7. You can find similar lists by doing a search for prefix and suffix activities on the internet and in Nation, I. S. P. 1984. *Vocabulary lists: words, affixes and stems.* English Language Institute, Victoria University of Wellington, Wellington. On this book's website, there are worksheets for students to work in pairs on prefixes. You can download copies of these charts.
8. This worksheet is based on prefix tables and a teaching idea from Nation, I. S. P. 1984. *Vocabulary lists: words, affixes and stems.* English Language Institute, Victoria University of Wellington, Wellington.
9. See this book's website at http://www.college.hmco.com/esl/students for links to crossword puzzles for vocabulary study.
10. For more examples of classroom activities using suffixes and prefixes, see Nation, 2001.
11. You can download copies of these charts from this book's website at http://www.college.hmco.com/esl/instructors
12. Schmitt, N. and C. Boyd-Zimmerman. 2002. Derivative word forms: What do learners know? *TESOL Quarterly, 36*(2), 145–172.
13. For more examples of word stems, see Nation, 2001.

Chapter 6

Indirect Learning Strategies

FEATURED IN THIS CHAPTER

- What are indirect strategies for learning vocabulary?
- How can learners learn academic vocabulary through reading widely?
- What kinds of reading can help develop academic vocabulary?
- What kinds of listening can help develop academic vocabulary?
- What does guessing the meaning of unknown words from context involve?

What Are Indirect Strategies for Learning Vocabulary?

Vocabulary can be learned in direct ways, through flash cards for example as we saw in Chapter 5. It can also be 'picked up' or learned through indirect methods such as reading. Indirect learning means that learners are not focussing their attention on *learning* words in or out of context. Instead, learners are engaged in understanding the *meaning* of words in context. That is, they are focussed mostly on the message.

How Can Learners Learn Academic Vocabulary Through Extensive Reading?

Extensive reading[1] is successfully and efficiently reading a wide range of books. What effect does reading have on vocabulary? There is evidence to show that extensive reading can contribute to vocabulary growth.[2] It is important that extensive reading takes place over a sustained period of time. In one study, the researchers estimated that learners who had been required to read widely gained approximately 3000 new words after just one semester.[3] These students scored significantly higher on the post-study vocabulary tests than did the other group who were in a regular program of English for Academic Purposes over the same amount of time.

As well as encouraging vocabulary growth, extensive reading has positive effects on writing including grammar, mechanical features of writing such as spelling and punctuation, and overall writing impression.[4] Learners need to read a great deal of material from a wide range of sources.[5] The more your learners read, the more words they will come across.

Things to keep in mind about extensive reading and vocabulary learning:

- Learners need to be informed about the importance of extensive reading for vocabulary learning.
- Students need to be referred back to the learning principles of repetition, spaced retrieval and frequency to help them understand how extensive reading fits into their vocabulary learning goals.
- The reading material should be interesting to the learners so they are encouraged to read.
- An easy rule of thumb to use when choosing texts is that learners should aim to read only books with five or so unknown words per page. They need to know about 99 words out every 100 on the page for successful extensive reading. If learners find the content interesting, then perhaps 97 words out of 100 would need to be known. To put it another way, in a passage of 1000 words, there could be 10 new words.
- Extensive reading has to work alongside direct learning of vocabulary.[6] Learners will do better if they include words they have met in their regular vocabulary learning routine. They could, for example, add the words to their vocabulary notebook or flash card set.

- Students should be encouraged to discuss with peers the work they are reading. Evidence shows that learners who read in English and then talked about the books in their first language made a great deal of progress in language development.[7] These learners did even better than those who also wrote about the books they were reading and those who read and wrote about the books and received feedback on their writing.[8]

What Kinds of Reading Can Help Develop Academic Vocabulary?

Academic words tend to occur most frequently in academic texts, as we have seen earlier in the introduction. The Academic Word List covers up to 10 percent of the words in an academic text.[9]

Many academic subject areas now have introductory textbooks that are useful for students planning to study at tertiary level. You may find that learners need to start with beginning academic material such as 'Dummies Guides' or simplified textbooks.

Newspapers contain a large number of academic words but the stories tend to be too short for extensive reading. You could ask learners to follow media stories over the course of weeks or months, thereby ensuring that key words are met over and over again.[10] This kind of reading is called 'narrow reading' rather than extensive reading. Interest levels can be kept high if the stories are selected personally by the students. Also, as learners become more familiar with the stories and the people involved, the problems associated with lower-frequency vocabulary might lessen.

A wide variety of general English-graded readers are available in bookstores and some are now online. Graded readers are books written with second-language speakers in mind[11] and are useful for developing the first 2,000 words of English. Academic-graded readers are now being developed to bridge the gap between easy reading materials and difficult authentic textbooks.

What Kinds of Listening Can Help Develop Academic Vocabulary?

Extensive listening is similar to extensive reading in a second language in that learners need to listen to a great deal of high-interest listening material at the right level. They need to listen for enjoyment and understanding. Learners also need to understand the purpose and scope of extended listening, and how it fits into their learning programme[12] (see the previous section on extensive reading).

- Link the academic listening materials to academic reading materials on the same or related topics, and you will be providing good opportunities for the repetition of words, for background knowledge to be activated and for learners to notice words in their context.
- Make sure learners have easy access to materials that are appropriate for their language level. Knowledge of up to 99 percent of words is a good amount because at this level learners do not have to rely on help such as dictionaries while they listen.

Talks and lectures on general academic subjects can be useful input for extensive listening.[13] For example, if you are working on a unit connected with money, you could invite an Economics specialist to speak to your class. Speakers need to be well-prepared for a nonspecialist audience. In practical terms, speakers can attend to academic vocabulary by:

- Providing a short abstract of the talk before class so learners can prepare for the listening experience by looking carefully at the target words.
- Thinking about the vocabulary they are going to use and how they will teach it if they think the learners will not know it well enough to understand it in a new context.
- Highlighting target words using visual aids such as Power Point, slides, pictures and overhead transparencies.

One very useful characteristic of listening is that one person's speaking is another person's listening. Discussions, role-plays, debates and formal talks between learners all provide extra material for listening. Learners will need time to talk about their listening with classmates. Talking about what they have heard might encourage learners:

- to notice the target words they have heard;
- to negotiate the meaning of the words they have heard;
- to focus on the target words for direct learning;
- to use the words they have been hearing as they talk.

Can you think of other sources of material that would be of high-interest and at the right level for easy listening for your students?

What Does the Strategy of Guessing the Meaning of Unknown Words from Context Involve?

Students can become better learners and users of words by direct training in how to handle unknown words in readings. A major feature of their academic study will be recognizing, figuring out and deciding how to learn new vocabulary in textbooks. The strategy called 'guessing meaning of words from context' may help learners to understand the meaning of unknown words when they come across them. It is aimed at helping learners to close the gap in their knowledge. Not all words, however, can be guessed from context.

Learners may choose to learn the words they have guessed. However, they will only do so as a conscious decision after they have finished reading. As we know, learners will have more chance of increasing their knowledge of a word if they study it directly.

Research shows that learners do not make many vocabulary gains through this strategy.[14] They will, however:

- develop their guessing skills in reading as word learners and word users;
- increase their awareness of words in context;
- improve their understanding of decisions they make while reading that affect their vocabulary learning.[15]

Steps in the Strategy

The guessing-meaning-from-context strategy has several steps. There are some variations that other people might use, but try the following steps from Nation[16] and see how they suit you and your learners.

> **Step 1:** Look at the grammar of the word. This means checking to see if it is a noun, a verb, an adjective or an adverb, for example. You can check that learners know these classes of words by writing some simple sentences on the board and asking learners to identify the grammar of each word. Here are some example sentences:
>
> I like bananas.[17]
> New Zealand is a lovely country.
>
> **Step 2:** Look at the words in the sentence that are connected with the unknown word. This means if the unknown word is a noun, what is the verb and/or adjective that goes with it? If it is a verb, is there an adverb or a noun that goes with it?
> **Step 3:** Look at the paragraph to see how the target word fits in. For example, can you find the word repeated elsewhere, a synonym, an antonym, a pronoun or even the meaning of the word explained somewhere else in the text?
> **Step 4:** Guess the word.
> **Step 5:** Put the guess into the sentence. Check to see that learners have matched the grammar of the guessed word to that of the unknown word. Check also that the sentence makes sense with the guess in it. If it doesn't, the learners need to make a decision—do they go back to step one in the strategy, or reach for a dictionary?

How Can You Introduce Learners to This Strategy?

You can start with a discussion on what to do with unknown words in texts. Learners usually have some strategies they use, such as ignoring unknown words, some sort of guessing strategy or using the dictionary.

- Introduce the guessing-meaning-from-context strategy steps to your students, making sure they understand that each part requires them to pay close attention to the word in its widening context.
- Encourage learners to use their knowledge of the world and the topic as resources to draw on.
- Model using the strategy and making sensible guesses based on classroom reading.

Trying Out Guessing-Meaning-from-Context

Here is a short text on a native bird of New Zealand, the Kiwi. Some words in the text have been underlined. Use the strategy steps to go through the text, guessing what the underlined words mean. Pretend you don't know the words and are approaching the text for the first time.

THE KIWI: WEIRD AND WONDERFUL[18]

Thanks to New Zealand's ancient isolation and lack of mammals, the kiwi evolved to occupy a habitat and lifestyle that elsewhere in the world is occupied by a mammal. It means that in many ways the kiwi is a very unbird-like bird. Its skin is tough as shoe-leather, its feathers are like hair, its bones are heavy, its wings end in a cat-like claw and its body temperature is 38° Celsius, lower than most other birds. While most birds depend on sight, the kiwi is one of the few birds with a highly developed sense of smell. At night, kiwi can be heard sniffing around in the dark.

Were some of the words easier to guess than others? Why would this be the case? Perhaps there are many unknown words in the text. In this case, the learners will be trying to guess too many words with not enough context. Practise this strategy only with easier texts (where 95–98 percent of the words are known), so learners will be reasonably successful at guessing.

How Can You Practise Guessing-Meaning-from-Context in Class?

You can practice guessing-meaning-from-context in almost any class. As long as there are not too many unknown words in the text, your learners should be able to apply the strategy.

It is helpful if the words are central to the text so the learners have to process them to understand the text well. Here are some basic steps for practising guessing-meaning-from-context:

1. You or your learners can highlight, underline or **bold** the words to work on in the text. Be careful not to number each of the words. If you do, it is likely the learners will refer to the words by the numbers, not by using the words themselves.

2. Have learners work in pairs initially and think aloud as they discuss the words. Have them make sure they are clear on the possible meanings and the clues in the text that helped them decide their guesses. If learners know the meaning of the highlighted word, have them identify the clues in the text that would have helped them guess the meaning.
3. Have a class feedback session where learners discuss how they came to their guesses and what clues they found in the text to help them.
4. Have learners review the strategy by explaining it to their partner, who makes sure the explanation is clear and correct. Or ask learners to teach the strategy to another learner outside the class.

Here are some key points to remember about guessing the meaning of unknown words in context.

- Students need to practise over and over again in short sessions.
- The number of unknown words in a text can severely affect a learner's ability to guess a word's meaning.
- The unknown words need to carry meaning in the text or be important to the text to make sure learners notice and focus on them.[19]
- Ideally, words would be repeated in a text so learners have more chances to pick up the meaning through several exposures.[20]
- Learners have to be involved in what is happening when they are guessing the meaning of a word.[21]
- The learners' background knowledge needs to be activated for successful guessing to take place.[22]
- Remember that this is not a vocabulary learning strategy but it can be used to teach students how to more effectively handle new words they encounter in their academic studies.

As with any strategy, it is the repetition and practise that help the learners to become more comfortable and able to apply the strategy in a new situation.

Endnotes

1. The website for this book has a link to the Extensive Reading Foundation website for useful information on starting a programme of extensive reading.
2. Elley, W., & F. Mangubhai. 1981. *The impact of a book flood in Fiji Primary Schools.* Wellington, New Zealand: New Zealand Council for Educational Research; Lao, C., & S. Krashen. 2000. The impact of popular literature study on literacy development in EFL: more evidence for the power of reading. *System, 28*, 261–270 and Day, R., & J. Bamford. 1998. *Extensive reading in the second language classroom.* Cambridge: Cambridge University Press.
3. Lao, C., & S. Krashen. 2000.
4. Mason, B., & S.Krashen. 1997. Extensive reading in an Asian context—an alternative view. *System, 25*(1), 91–102.
5. Day, R., & J. Bamford. 1998. *Extensive reading in the second language classroom.* Cambridge: Cambridge University Press.
6. Nation, P. 2001. *Learning vocabulary in another language.* Cambridge: Cambridge University Press. See especially page 156.
7. Mason, B., & S. Krashen. 1997.
8. Mason, B., & S. Krashen. 1997.
9. Coxhead, A. 2000. A new academic word list. *TESOL Quarterly, 34*(2), 213–238.
10. Schmitt, R., & R. Carter. 2000. The lexical advantages of narrow reading for second language learners. *TESOL Journal, 9*(1), 4–9.
11. Check the websites of major publishers in the field of English as a Second Language (ESOL/ESL) for their lists of graded readers.
12. See *Essentials of teaching academic oral communication* by John Murphy in this Houghton Mifflin series for more on academic listening and vocabulary.
13. I first saw this at Victoria University of Wellington, New Zealand.
14. For a discussion of the pros and cons of guessing-meaning-from-context, see Nation, 2001, especially pages 232–262.
15. For more on the research behind guessing-meaning-from-context and connecting it to your classroom, see Folse, K. 2004. *Vocabulary myths.* Ann Arbor: University of Michigan Press, pages 71–84.
16. Nation. 2001.
17. I like bananas. (I = pronoun, like = verb, bananas = noun). New Zealand is a lovely country. (New Zealand = noun, is = verb, a = article, lovely = adjective, country = noun).
18. The Kiwi, weird and wonderful. Available at http://www.kiwirecovery.org.nz/Kiwi/AboutTheBird/WeirdAndWonderful/ on 9 December 2003.

19. Sternburg, R. 1987. Most vocabulary is learned from context. In McKeown, M., & M. Curtis (Eds.). *The nature of vocabulary acquisition* (pp. 89–105). Hillsdale, NJ: Lawrence Erlbaum.

20. Paribakht, T., & M. Wesche. 1997. Vocabulary enhancement activities and reading for meaning in second language vocabulary acquisition. In Coady, J. & T. Huckin. (Eds.) *Second Language Acquisition* (pp. 174–200). Cambridge: Cambridge University Press.

21. Paribakht & Wesche. 1997.

22. Sternburg, R. 1987. Most vocabulary is learned from context. In McKeown, M. & M. Curtis. *The nature of vocabulary acquisition* (pp. 89–105). Hillsdale, NJ: Lawrence Erlbaum.

Chapter **7**

Teaching the Core Meaning of Words, Using Dictionaries and Adapting Vocabulary Notebooks

FEATURED IN THIS CHAPTER

- How can learning a word's core meaning help with learning academic words?
- How can we use dictionaries to learn academic vocabulary?
- What are some ways of using vocabulary notebooks to learn academic vocabulary?

In this chapter, we will look at more strategies for learning academic vocabulary. The first, learning the core meaning of an academic word, encourages learners to look for connections between word meanings. The second strategy is using dictionaries to learn vocabulary. Finally, we will look at ways to adapt vocabulary notebooks to make them more effective.

How Can Learning the Core Meaning of an Academic Word Help with Learning?

Finding the main or core meaning of the word[1] involves looking for similarities, not differences, in a word's meaning. It is worth looking at this concept as it is a good way to encourage learners to think deeply about the meaning of a word.

Here is an example of trying to find the core meaning of a word.

> **According to *The American Heritage English as a Second Language Dictionary*,[2] *consider* has several meanings including:**
>
> - **Think carefully about something**, as in *consider what someone has said*.
> - **Believe something to be**, as in *consider something to be beautiful*.
> - **Be thoughtful** as in *consider other people's feelings*.
>
> Looking at these meanings, what would you *consider* to be the central or core meaning of *consider*?

You might answer that the core meaning of *consider* is something about thinking deeply or carefully about something. Would you teach each of the word's meanings separately, or is there a way to teach the central meaning so learners will be able to work out the meaning of *consider* when they meet it in a slightly new context?

Here is another example of an activity that encourages learners to look for the core meaning of a word.[3]

consistent/ kən sĭs′ tənt/adjective	consistent/ kən sĭs′ tənt/adjective	What is the core meaning of this word?
Someone who is **consistent** always behaves in the same way, has the same attitudes towards people or things, or achieves the same level of success in something. *Becker has never been the most consistent of players anyway . . . his consistent support of free trade.* **Is there anyone you know who has consistent good luck?**	If one fact or idea is **consistent** with another, they do not contradict each other. *This result is consistent with the findings of another study . . . New goals are not always consistent with the old ones.* **Tom found that studying vocabulary each night for three hours increased his vocabulary by over 40 percent. Is this consistent with your experience?**	

Your answer might be '*something which is consistent remains basically the same.*' The thinking and interaction about the vocabulary between students is important. Act as a consultant who listens to what learners think is the central meaning and then confirm their ideas or guide their thinking if they are slightly off track. Visser showed that learners in her study were correct with their guesses up to 95 percent of the time.[4] Here are some more suggestions on ways of teaching the core meanings of words:

- Have students look in a dictionary at the individual meanings under a headword and find a central meaning connecting all the meanings.
- Ask students to decide the core meaning of a word based on several examples of the word in context.

How Can We Use Dictionaries for Learning Academic Vocabulary?

Dictionaries have a lot more to offer vocabulary learning than just meanings. Using a dictionary well is a skill all learners need to develop.[5] Learners need help in finding ways to find and use to their advantage the information a dictionary offers.

Modern dictionaries take factors such as frequency of words into account when selecting items for inclusion. They try to be user-friendly by using the first 2,000 words of English for writing definitions and show examples of the words in use.[6] Some dictionaries are now available online.

Many learners use electronic dictionaries regularly and can successfuly find one-to-one translations. Most learners prefer to use a bilingual dictionary.[7] Electronic dictionaries are fine for a quick check of understanding, but these dictionaries as yet have not been developed in a principled way. That is, unlike paper dictionaries, they do not help with frequency, often do not include multiple meanings for words with more than one meaning and do not take into account word family formation. Electronic dictionaries will continue to develop, and if used well, can become good learning tools.

Like other strategies, learners need to learn and practice dictionary skills to become better able to use the reference materials well.[8] The first thing, however, is for you and your learners to decide which dictionary or dictionaries will suit your needs best.

Choosing a Dictionary

Choosing the right dictionary is a difficult task. It may be that learners actually need several dictionaries to support their language learning. A simple way to encourage learners to explore the range and types of dictionaries, online, on CD-ROM or printed, is to survey the dictionaries. Schools and local libraries, as well as teachers and institutions, should have a good range of dictionaries to work with. You could always ask other successful language learners which dictionaries they use and how they use them. This survey may bring up a range of interesting topics and strategy-based discussions on dictionaries, including modeling good dictionary skills.

Strategy-Training with Dictionary Use

Think about what learners have to do when they look up words in a dictionary. They need to:

- search for the right word;
- find the right meaning for a word by evaluating other entries if it has more than one main meaning;
- understand the coding in the dictionary;
- understand that some words (e.g., plural nouns, superlatives, multi-word units and word family members) might not be in the dictionary as a head word. This means you have to look for the word under another heading.[9]

You can design dictionary tasks around any other skills or language work your learners are doing in or outside class. For example, in preparation for a reading, writing, listening or speaking class, your learners could look up words for meanings, pronunciation, common collocations or word stress.

Looking up the word and then using it leads to greater retention than just reading.[10] Here are some more ideas you could try in class.

- Working with the signs and codes in dictionaries to develop skills in interpreting quickly what they mean. For example, if you are working with *The American Heritage English as a Second Language Dictionary*, what do the superscript numbers mean beside a head-word entry?[11]
- Focussing on grammatical patterns in dictionary entries,[12] such as verbs followed by verb + ing as in *I enjoy doing homework.*
- Using information such as synonyms and homonyms in dictionary entries. For example, in *The American Heritage English as a Second Language Dictionary* under the entry for *method*, learners will find a box of synonyms or words that have a similar meaning, including *system*, *routine* and *manner*. Each word is then explained in more detail with an example of the word in use.[13]
- Using information in a dictionary to help with word parts. For example, the entry for *micro* in the *The American Heritage English as a Second Language Dictionary* tells the learner that this is a prefix and it means *small or smaller*. Following the entry is a word building section where *micro* is explained in more detail with examples.[14]

■ Cross-referencing words with similar meanings to establish differences in use, for example, contrasting *paradigm*, *principle* and *rule*. Be careful with learners doing this however, as they may get confused between meanings. Establish the most frequent word first for learners before asking them to compare one word with a new word to help them avoid interference between the words.

Modeling the process of consulting a dictionary is important. Bring dictionaries to class or make sure there are some already there and encourage learners to bring them along too.

Using the dictionary to look up words is only one part of learning a word. Learners and teachers need to make sure there are many opportunities for encountering the words again, to use the words in speaking and writing and to gain feedback on their use. Here are some points to remember about dictionaries and vocabulary.

■ One meeting with a word is just the first step towards learning the word.
■ More exposures to the word in different contexts will deepen learners' knowledge as long as they notice the word and process it.
■ Spaced retrieval (see the principles in Chapter 2) has a large part to play in dictionary use. A learner who looks up a word but does nothing with it will not remember it and will need to look it up again.
■ Direct learning strategies such as putting the word in a vocabulary notebook, making a flash card, looking for it in other contexts, trying to use it in writing and speaking will increase learners' chances of learning the word.
■ Learners need training and support with dictionary use to be more effective, more efficient and to gain more knowledge from them.[15]

What if you want to move learners away from constant dictionary use? You could introduce extensive reading into the language program (see Chapter 6) or introduce an intensive program on dictionary work and use.[16]

What Are Some Ways of Using Vocabulary Notebooks for Learning Academic Vocabulary?

I had a vocabulary notebook when I was studying French at high school. I kept very careful records of new words from class. Each word was put in an old address book that had pages with letters of the alphabet on them. On the left was the word in French. On the right was the word in English. With nouns I recorded whether I needed to use *la* or *le* with them and the plural form also. I revised my words by running my eye from the key word to the translation. Seeing the translation seemed to confirm to me that I knew the words. When it came to using the words in speaking or writing however, I could never quite remember the words on the page as clearly as when I had looked at them last. Does this sound familiar?

What would I do now to make my vocabulary notebook more effective?

- Organise my word entries into semantic maps to help develop my knowledge of the concepts around words.
- Think carefully about where and how to enter words into my notebook so that the connections between words would be clear and I would know where to find the words quickly.
- Work with the idea that words occur with other words and that collocations are an important part of learning about a word.
- Think about ways to avoid interference between words that look similar or are opposites.
- Incorporate the idea of frequency by ranking words in order of frequency or learning the more frequent items first.
- Make the entries rich by including more information than just the grammatical focus. Include information about the words, for example, their pronunciation, common collocations, word family members, word stress and any key word that helps connect the meaning and the sound.
- Use retrieval more often in my learning, rather than just looking at the word in French and doing an immediate check with the English word along the same line.
- Develop a system for recording entries that reflect the incremental word knowledge I gain as I encounter them or try to use them in speaking or writing.[17]

- Ensure that I have a system for recording my attempts to use the words and analyzing the feedback I receive.
- Ask other learners how they organise their vocabulary notebooks and try to find other ways of learning that support my own system.

You might discuss vocabulary notebooks in class and experiment with different ways to keep notebooks.

Here is an example of a vocabulary notebook that I have seen many learners use.[18] This sample is not to scale. You can see that there are a number of aspects of word knowledge in the example.

Example of a Vocabulary Notebook

Word	Meaning (first or second language?)	Pron.	Original sentence	Word family member	Common collocations	Your own Sentence

There is room for learners to record their entries and add information about the words as they develop their knowledge. Normally this page would be landscape allowing more room for learners to write. Learners who successfully used this method added to their notebook entries when they noticed or found something new about a word. Put another way, these learners worked incrementally on their vocabulary knowledge, rather than trying to fill all the gaps and learn all the aspects of a word all at once.

One reason why some learners have been unsuccessful with recording words is they have spent a lot of time transferring information from a dictionary directly onto the page. These learners did not process the information in a meaningful way or try to use the words in their speaking or writing. They often relied heavily on their first-language translation of the words. Perhaps one of the best ways to help learners avoid these traps is to discuss them, try to find ways together to get around them and focus on the real task at hand—learning vocabulary.

Endnotes

1. Visser, A. 1989. Learning core meanings. *Guidelines, 11* (2), 10–17.
2. *The American Heritage English as a second language dictionary*. 1998. Boston: Houghton Mifflin. (p. 188.)
3. I adapted this example from the work of Visser, A. 1989. Learning core meanings. *Guidelines, 11* (2), 10–17. The dictionary entry comes from Sinclair, J. (Ed.) 2001. *Collins COBUILD Dictionary for advanced learners*. London : Collins. Thank you to Michelle Strand and Judith Mason for developing these exercises with me.
4. Visser. 1989.
5. See Folse, K. 2004. *Vocabulary myths*. Ann Arbor: University of Michigan Press, pages 107–126 for more on dictionaries and vocabulary learning.
6. For an excellent discussion of learners and dictionary use, skills, and developing language and dictionary skills in second-language learners, see Nation, P. 2001. *Learning vocabulary in another language*. Cambridge: Cambridge University Press. See especially pages 282–299.
7. Laufer, B., & M. Kimmel. 1997. Bilingual dictionaries: How learners really use them. *System 25*, 361–369.
8. Carrell, P., & W. Grabe. 2002. Reading. In Schmitt, N. (Ed.) *Introduction to applied linguistics*. Arnold: London. See especially page 242.
9. Hulstijn, J. 1993. When do foreign-language readers look up the meaning of unfamiliar words? The influence of task and learner variables. *Modern Language Journal 77*, 139–147.
10. Laufer, B. 2002. Vocabulary acquisition in a second language: Do learners really acquire most vocabulary by reading? Some empirical evidence. *The Canadian Modern Language Review 59* (4), 567–587.
11. The superscript numbers in *The American Heritage English as a second language dictionary* indicate that the head word is a homograph. In other words, these words have the same spelling but not the same meaning. *The American Heritage English as a second language dictionary*. 1998. Boston: Houghton Mifflin. See page xi for an explanation of their symbol system.
12. Wright, J. 1998. *Dictionaries*. Oxford: Oxford University Press.
13. *The American Heritage English as a second language dictionary*. 1998. Boston: Houghton Mifflin. Page 553.
14. *The American Heritage English as a second language dictionary*. 1998. Boston: Houghton Mifflin. Page 554.
15. For more ideas on using dictionaries in class and learner training in dictionary use, see Wright, J. 1998. *Dictionaries*. Oxford: Oxford University Press; Thornbury, S. 2002. *How to teach vocabulary*. Longman: Harlow, Essex; and Nation, P. 2001. *Learning vocabulary in another language*. Cambridge: Cambridge University Press.

16. Nuttall, C. 1996. *Teaching reading skills in a foreign language*. Hong Kong: Macmillan Heinemann. See especially page 62.
17. Schmitt, N., & D. Schmitt. 1995. Vocabulary notebooks: Theoretical underpinnings and practical suggestions. *ELTJ 49* (2), 133–143.
18. I first saw a notebook entry like this in the School of Linguistics and Applied Language Studies at Victoria University of Wellington.

Part **3**

Developing Vocabulary Through Skills-Based Classroom Work

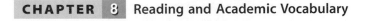

Chapter **8**

Reading and Academic Vocabulary

In Chapter 6 we looked at reading extensively to learn vocabulary. In this chapter, we will look at reading intensively and learning vocabulary.[1] We will start by examining texts to see which are more suitable for students with academic purposes. Then we will move onto noticing language in context with a focus on vocabulary.

Reading and Vocabulary

Learning through reading is a natural way to acquire vocabulary, as long as the reading materials are within learners' level of understanding. There are three key points to reading for the purpose of learning academic vocabulary.

- The more you read, the better your reading and the bigger your vocabulary.
- The bigger your vocabulary, the more you can read.
- Reading meets several of the principles of effective vocabulary learning that we looked at in Chapter 2.
    - One principle, repetition, can be met through meeting the same word or words in a text several times, reading the same text several times or reading two or more texts in the same subject area.
    - Retrieval comes from meeting the words in context and trying to recall their meaning while reading.
    - Generation comes from meeting the words in new contexts.

What Should We Keep in Mind When Selecting Academic Texts to Read?

A text with too many difficult words or which is beyond learners' ablility puts a great deal of strain on them. Imagine reading a text with more than 50 percent of the words unknown to you. You would spend more time looking up the words than reading. You would also spend more time wishing you were doing something else than 'reading' this text.

Learners need to be able to understand the meaning of at least 95 percent to 98 percent of the words in the text.[2] For intensive reading the amount can be slightly below 95 percent, but there is little research evidence that is more specific. This is because it is difficult to measure word knowledge and successful reading without taking other factors into account, such as the readers' individual characteristics, time allowed and available resources. It is also difficult to accurately predict how much of a text is unknown.

How Can You Find Out How Many Unknown Words Are in Texts?

As we noted, it can be difficult to find out what vocabulary is unknown in a text. You can use your judgment of where your learners are at, but you may run into several different types of problems using intuition. These problems may include:

- If too much time has passed between meetings with the words, then learners are more likely to have completely or partially forgotten them.
- A different context or collocations in a text may be new to the students. For example, a word such as *sanction* might be presented with a completely new meaning.
- Learners may not know the words particularly well. Like learning any new skill, it takes time, repetition, patience, involvement and salience for vocabulary to become well-known and useful in another language.

Luckily there are more and more tools becoming available for searching text for words and classifying or highlighting them as possible unknown words. Like any tool, however, they need to be used carefully and their findings interpreted with your class and the students' needs in mind. Here are some suggestions.

- Use Internet-based computer programs or websites. For example, by running your texts through the Range Programme,[3] you can find out how many words come from the first and second thousand word lists and the AWL. You will also find out how many words in the text do not come from any of these lists.
- Ask a learner to underline all the words he or she knows in a text.
- Ask learners to individually report on how many words on a page they recognize and know well.

What Kinds of Texts Do Students Need to Read to Get Exposure to Academic Language?

Students need to read a lot so they encounter the words many times in context to be able to cement the words in their minds. Each new meeting with a word should reinforce its familiarity and might bring some new knowledge to further fill the knowledge gap about it. For example, a learner might learn a new collocation for the word, may meet a new member of the word family, or may notice the spelling. See Chapter 6 for more on vocabulary and extensive reading.

We know they need to read, but what do they need to read? Students need to read the right sort of material for their purpose. Some texts do not have many academic words in them. I reported in my study of academic vocabulary in written texts that on average, the AWL made up 10 percent of a body of texts made up of 3,500,000 running words from 28 different academic subject areas.[4]

In the same study, I reported that in a large corpus of fiction texts, the AWL made up only 1.4 percent of the words in the texts. Compare the 10 percent for academic texts and 1.4 percent for fiction, with the AWL making up 4.5 percent of words in newspapers, and you can see that the type of text has an enormous effect on the kinds of words used.

To illustrate this point, we compare a short text from Rudyard Kipling's *The Jungle Book*[5] with an academic accounting text. You can see big differences in the vocabulary.

In the two texts, the words have been coded in the following way:

1. Normal font = first 2,000 words
2. *Bold italics* = AWL words
3. Underlined = words not in the first 2,000 or in the AWL

Text One: From *The Jungle Book*	Text Two: From a written accounting text
It was seven o'clock of a very warm evening in the Seeonee hills when Father Wolf woke up from his day's rest, scratched himself, yawned, and spread out his paws one after the other to get rid of the sleepy feeling in their tips.[6] (44 words)	This report provides substantive *evidence* of a different record of events and *processes* in New Zealand surrounding the failure of the current cost accounting (CCA) standard in New Zealand, and in particular examines the differences between these events in New Zealand and the United Kingdom.[7] (45 words)

If we compare the two texts, what can we see?

- The words from the first 2,000 words of English occur often in both texts. This means that readers who read fiction and academic texts need these high-frequency words first.
- *The Jungle Book* text has, on the whole, many shorter words than the academic text. You can see this by the way the academic text takes up more room on the page than the fiction text does.
- The academic text has a high proportion of AWL words but the fiction text contains none. There are two main points to consider when we think of this:
  - Academic words are much more likely to occur in the academic text than in the fiction text.
  - We know these academic words (and others from the AWL) will also occur in other academic texts, not just in the field of commerce, but also in education, sociology, biology, physics, law, psychology, chemistry and geography, to name a few.[8]
- The words that do not occur in any list are lower-frequency words. See the section at the end of this chapter on dealing with lower-frequency words.

Newspapers can be a good source of suitable reading because academic words tend to occur in them. However, newspaper stories can cause some problems if they are very short or on a topic that learners know very little about. One way around this problem is by asking learners to identify topics in the news that they would be interested in following and set up a reading program that encourages searching for developments in those stories.[9]

So, there are several answers to the question 'What kinds of texts do students need to read to get exposure to academic language?'

1. Texts they can handle. That is, texts without too many unknown words.
2. Texts with an academic topic or focus. Fiction texts tend not to contain significant numbers of academic words.

Once the reading materials are selected, turn your attention to connecting reading with vocabulary teaching and learning. A key part of this is training learners to become active readers with highly tuned and independent vocabulary learning systems.

How Can We Deal with Subject-Specific Academic Vocabulary and Lower–Frequency Words?

Subject-Specific Vocabulary

Subject-specific words are strongly connected to an area of study such as economics, biology or marketing. The phrase *Current Cost Accounting (CCA)* in the accounting text all clearly relate to the subject of accounting and to the topic of the article, *current cost accounting*. These words can be called 'subject-specific' or 'technical' vocabulary. For some learners, these subject-specific words are important because they will be needed in future studies.

Subject-specific or technical vocabulary may cause problems for several reasons.

- Learners may not know subject-specific vocabulary well.[10]
- Subject-specific words may account for a great number of the words in a text.[11]
- Subject-specific words may be conceptually loaded. That is, learners have to learn new concepts at the same time as they are learning the new words.

- Some subject-specific words may be well-known to students as part of their general or academic vocabulary, but these words take on a particular meaning when used in a different context. For example, *significant* takes on a new meaning when it is used in statistics.

What can you do to help learners with subject-specific vocabulary?

- Learners could build their own lists of useful technical words they encounter during their reading.
- Subject-specific words could form a special part of a targeted vocabulary learning program. Learners would practice strategies for learning these words.
- Learners may find reading in the subject area helps them with these words, because the textbooks should contain the target words in context.
- Some subjects have dictionaries to help with learning key words and concepts.

Lower-Frequency Vocabulary

Lower-frequency words are generally words that occur in only a few texts. They tend not to occur with high frequency across a wide variety of texts. There are lists of lower-frequency words available,[12] but it is better to focus valuable learning and teaching time on higher-frequency items. Nation[13] suggests that training learners to deal with these lower-frequency words through strategies such as guessing meaning from context (see Chapter 6) is a more effective use of time.

Here are some more key points about lower-frequency words:

- Lower-frequency words may occur more often in one text than another. For example, *Zealand* is not likely to come up in *The Jungle Book*, just as *wolf* would probably not be used in an academic accounting text.
- Some words in the texts above, such as *jungle* might not seem to be lower frequency compared to words like *failure*. The reason why these words are lower frequency is the selection criteria used when the first 2,000 word list and the AWL were compiled. West[14] used six selection criteria to create his General Service List of the

first 2,000 words. The criteria included *frequency*, *ease of learning* and *cover*. By *cover*, West meant that if a selected word was doing the job of another word, then only one of the words went on the list. It is for this reason that *work* is one of the first 2,000 words but *job* is on the AWL.

- Words that are low frequency for some people may well be high frequency for others. If you come from *New Zealand*, then *Zealand* will be a high-frequency word for you because it is part of the name of your country.
- Abbreviations, such as *CCA* in the accounting text, can be low-frequency words.

Remember, these lower-frequency words may not be worth learners learning or teachers teaching because they will probably not be needed after students finish the text. Because of this, it is important to teach students strategies for dealing with them as they read.[15]

Endnotes

1. See the Reading books in this Houghton Mifflin series for an integrated approach to reading and vocabulary for academic purposes with texts and exercises.
2. For more on reading and vocabulary, see Nation, P. 2001. *Learning vocabulary in another language*. Cambridge: Cambridge University Press.
3. Range is available online from Paul Nation's website; there's a link to that website from this book's website at http://www.college.hmco.com/esl/instructors. From Nation's site, you can download the programme and run it on PCs. Instructions are part of the programme. Your texts need to be available on the computer.
4. Coxhead, A. 2000. A new academic word list. *TESOL Quarterly 34*(2), 213–238.
5. I chose the Kipling text as an example because it is readily available and will hopefully be easily recognisable to readers. Kipling, R. *The jungle book*. Downloaded from Project Gutenberg http://www.ibiblio.org/gutenberg/etext95/jnglb10.txt on Nov. 11, 2003.
6. Kipling, R. *The jungle book*. Downloaded from Project Gutenberg http://www.ibiblio.org/gutenberg/etext95/jnglb10.txt on Nov. 11, 2003.
7. Baskerville, R. 1996. The current cost debate: a re-examination of the significance of exogenous events in the failure of the CCA standard in New Zealand and the United Kingdom. Draft paper.
8. Coxhead, 2000.

9. I first learned of this idea from Alison Hamilton-Jenkins and Moina Simcock at Victoria University of Wellington, New Zealand. See also Schmitt, R., & R. Carter. 2000. The lexical advantages of narrow reading for second language learners, *TESOL Journal, 9*(1), 4–9.

10. Liu, J., & H. Nesi. 1999. Are we teaching the right words? A study of students' receptive knowledge of two types of vocabulary: 'subtechnical' and 'technical. In H. Bool & P. Luford (Eds.) *Academic standards and expectations: the role of EAP*. Nottingham: Nottingham University Press.

11. Chung, T., and P. Nation. 2003. Technical vocabulary in specialised texts. *Reading in a foreign language, 15*(2), 103–116.

12. Thorndike, E. L., & I. Lorge. 1944. *The teacher's word book of 30,000 words*. New York: Teachers College, Columbia University.

13. Nation, P. 2001. *Learning vocabulary in another language*. Cambridge: Cambridge University Press.

14. West, M. 1953. *A general service list of English words*. London: Longman, Green and Co.

15. Nation, P. 2001.

Chapter **9**

Academic Vocabulary in Reading Activities

FEATURED IN THIS CHAPTER

- How can we train students to notice academic vocabulary when they are reading?
- What classroom activities may help students focus on academic vocabulary before reading?
- What classroom activities may help students focus on academic vocabulary after reading?

In Chapter 8 we looked at reading and academic vocabulary in general. In this chapter, we will focus on activities you might be able to use in class to help develop your students' knowledge of academic vocabulary. We will start with training students to notice these words when they are reading and then we will move on to activities you can use both before and after reading.

How Can We Train Students to Notice Academic Vocabulary When They Are Reading?

There are many ways to draw a learner's attention to a word in a text.

- Highlight the target words by using **bold**, *italics*, underlining, highlighting, boxing, or circling, for example. You could use the AWL Highlighter website by Sandra Haywood to find and highlight the AWL words in the passages you are using.[1]
- Have students look for the target words in the text and highlight them in a way that is relevant to them. Here are several ways to do this:
  - In a pre-reading vocabulary brainstorm, have learners collect in two minutes all the words they know in relation to the topic. You can add the target words from the text during the brainstorm. Learners then skim the text looking for all the words from the brainstorm.
  - Direct the learners to the words you want them to notice by saying 'Look at the fourth word in paragraph three. Does anyone recognise this word?' You could direct more questions such as:
    - *Have you seen this word before?*
    - *What do you think the word means?*
    - *What other words in the sentence connect with this word?*
    - *Does this word occur anywhere else in the text?*
  - Devise a pre-reading discussion task involving the key words whereby the learners have to negotiate the word's meaning to complete the task. Research by Newton[2] shows that learners can make gains in learning vocabulary through negotiating vocabulary items in tasks. For example, you could design pre-reading discussion questions using some of the academic vocabulary from the text your students are about to read. Example discussion questions based on an accounting text[3] might be:
    - What is the primary way your country earns export dollars, to which countries and how do you think it could expand its markets in the future?
    - What could be the *primary* causes of a country's drop in export earnings? What fundamental changes have taken place in your country in the last 10 years in terms of technology, education and finance?

- What **research** methods might you use if you had to investigate accounting standards in two different countries? Are there any possible difficulties you can see in comparing two systems?

What Classroom Activities May Help Students Focus on Academic Vocabulary Before Reading?

Let's assume you have a text for intensive reading, you have identified the key words central to the meaning of the text and the words are important not only for today's class but also for future learning. Here are some activities you could use before reading that need very few materials and little time to set up.[4]

- Matching meanings and words using flash cards. Ask your learners to prepare one set of flash cards with academic words on them and another set with the meanings. They can swap sets of cards with other learners for extra practice in matching words and meanings. Having learners prepare the cards may help them learn the words they are focussing on.
- Having learners work on what they already know about the key words and their collocates by preparing matching activities for others in the class.
- Discussing the topic of the reading and brainstorming words the learners already know. You can use this opportunity to bring up the key words you want to highlight.
- Creating some discussion questions that include the key words and having learners discuss the questions, with a focus on negotiating the meanings.
- Pooling the expertise of the class through activities such as providing learners with the key words on slips of paper or dictating them so students can write them on small pieces of paper. Learners then individually separate the words into two piles—words they know and words they do not know. They then mix around the class, looking for learners who can tell them more about the words they don't know and helping others with their unknown words. If you use this activity, it is important to further check to make sure everyone has gained a clear picture of the meanings, the spelling, possible collocations and other aspects of the words.

- Developing quizzes whereby learners ask each other about different aspects of the words, with each student acting as an expert on a word they have studied before class. For example, you could have them asking questions such as:
  - This is the word, what is the meaning?
  - This is the word, what is the spelling?
  - This is the spelling, what is the word?
  - The word is X, what is a common collocation?
  - Can you put X into a sentence?
- Using the words in a strategy-training exercise before class to give learners some exposure before they start to focus on the words in a new and more meaningful way. For example, you could work on guessing meaning from context, using the key word technique or analyzing word parts of the key words.

What Classroom Activities May Help Students Focus on Academic Vocabulary after Reading?

Learners who focus on unknown words after reading will gain more in the long-term than those who just read.[5] This is because they will meet the words more often and will be thinking about them carefully. Learners need encouragement to think deeply about words and make connections between words in context. Activities that foster deeper thinking include:

- Evaluation tasks whereby learners make choices between words, for example, to complete a gap-fill summary with words from the text. If you design the summaries to include the words you want the learners to focus on, you will increase the likelihood of noticing and processing.
- Read and retell activities in which learners retell what they have read. They can refer to the original text as they retell, plan a short talk referring to notes they made on the text or not refer to the original text at all. Joe[6] found in her study that learners who did not refer to their text produced more of the target language than learners who did.
- Ranking activities in which students put words in order based on

various criteria. This task requires learners to think carefully about the words they have focussed on in the text. Again, it is vital that the target words are part of the ranking activity so that noticing can take place.[7] What can learners rank in a text?

- The ideas in order of importance.
- The target words according to how central they are to the main ideas.
- The ideas in the sequence of events.
- The learners' responses to ideas in the text according to how strongly they feel about them.

- Self-evaluating activities whereby learners select words from the text that they think are important to learn. Ask them why these words are important and how they plan to make them part of their vocabulary.
- Encouraging learners to find the gaps in their knowledge about the target words and to find ways to fill those gaps. They could do this by:
  - Studying the words by looking to see what collocations occur with them in the text.
  - Exploring a dictionary for any missing information such as whether the word is a countable or uncountable noun, its pronunciation, its use in common expressions or its collocations.
  - Finding out whether a word's new meaning is frequent or just used in certain contexts.
  - Identifying resources they can use to help them fill the gaps. The resources might be:
    - other learners in and out of the classroom;
    - the text used in class;
    - dictionaries;
    - the Internet;
    - other texts on similar topics that have the same words in them;
    - teachers and other high level users of the language they are learning. Can you think of any others?

Learning a little bit about words regularly is more effective than cramming a lot of detail. Cramming tends to lead to early forgetting. This is because the short-term memory cannot hold a lot of information for a long time. If learners do not refresh their learning with spaced repetition and retrieval, they will soon find they no longer remember much about the target words.

One final thing to remember is that learners need to read and then do something with the target words. These activities could include writing original sentences, doing additional vocabulary work, or speaking or writing the words in a similar context. These further activities help the process of acquisition.[8]

Endnotes

1. The AWL Highlighter by Sandra Haywood is available through the links provided on the website for this book at http://www.college.hmco.com/esl/instructors or at http://www.nottingham.ac.uk/~alzsh3/acvocab/awlhighlighter.htm.

2. Newton, J. 1993. *Task-based interaction among adult learners of English and its role in second languages development.* Unpublished Ph.D. thesis. Wellington: Victoria University of Wellington.

3. Baskerville, R. 1996. The current cost debate: a re-examiniation of the significance of exogenous events in the failure of the CCA standard in New Zealand and the United Kingdom. Draft paper.

4. These are only a few suggestions. For more activities, exercises and suggestions see the *Essentials of teaching academic reading* by Laura Walsh and Sharon Seymour in this Houghton Mifflin series.

5. See Paribakht, T., & M. Wesche. 1997. Vocabulary enhancement activities and reading for meaning in second language vocabulary acquisition. In Coady, J. and T. Huckin. (Eds.) *Second language acquisition.* Cambridge: Cambridge University Press. See also Laufer, B. 2001. Reading, word-focused activities and incidental vocabulary acquisition in a second language. *Prospect, 16*(3), 44–54.

6. Joe, A. 1994. *The effect of text-based tasks on incidental vocabulary learning.* Unpublished MA thesis. Wellington: Victoria University of Wellington.

7. Newton, 1995.

8. Laufer, B. 2001. Reading, word-focused activities and incidental vocabulary acquisition in a second language. *Prospect, 16*(3), 44–54.

Chapter **10**

Listening and Academic Vocabulary

FEATURED IN THIS CHAPTER

- Is it possible to learn academic vocabulary through listening?
- How can you build repetition and spaced retrieval into listening activities?
- How can we help learners to recognise academic words when they are spoken?
- Why is activating background knowledge important for listening and academic vocabulary?

Students I meet often consider listening one of the more difficult skills. They say that vocabulary is the cause of many of their problems, along with the fact that when listening, you only get one chance to catch what is being said. In this chapter, we will look at learning vocabulary through listening and trying to ensure that principles of vocabulary learning are included in listening tasks. We will also look at making the connection between the written and spoken words and why background knowledge can make a big difference in a learner's comprehension when listening.

Is It Possible to Learn Academic Vocabulary Through Listening?

The answer to this question is 'yes, but.' There are several reasons for saying 'yes,' and many reasons for saying 'but.' First, it seems there is a strong connection between having a high level of proficiency—being able to understand more[1]—and doing well in listening and reading tasks. This is also true of listening in an academic environment.[2] It also seems that highly proficient learners, while they understand more initially, tend to forget the words they have picked up in listening faster than students with lower proficiency.[3] Perhaps lower-proficiency learners have to work harder to understand new words, and their hard work pays off with a stronger learning connection.

There are a number of other considerations in answering the question of whether learners can learn vocabulary through listening. They are:

- What the learners are listening to needs to be at the right level for them to understand it.[4] If there are many unknown words in a passage, your learners will struggle to even make basic sense of what they are hearing.
- Listening and vocabulary need to be well supported by teachers and the learning environment. By this I mean that it must be clear to everyone that learning vocabulary is a central focus of the listening activity. Later in this chapter we will look at ways to approach teaching and learning vocabulary in listening tasks.
- Interesting materials make for more interested listeners.[5] Think about it this way—if you were learning another language, what would you prefer to listen to?[6]
- As with all learning, repetition is important. Whenever possible, encourage learners to listen several times to a passage. They could listen for different purposes each time.
- The key words need to be central to a passage's meaning in order for learners to notice and process them.
- Wider exposure to the words in other contexts will have a stronger effect on learning.[7]
- Listening alone will not help much with learning vocabulary. Words need to be focused on. When it comes to listening and vocabulary, there are many aspects of the words to work with, for example, their

meaning, sound, pronunciation, stress, and collocations. You don't need to work on all these aspects at once. Remember that learning vocabulary is an incremental process.

- It is important to remind learners that learning vocabulary through listening requires careful attention and specific follow-up.
- Lastly, learners need to spend considerable time listening and it would be ideal if the material is easily understood and of high interest.[8]

Let's move on and look at how to ensure that listening activities designed for the classroom can be created with vocabulary learning principles in mind.

How Can You Build Repetition and Spaced Retrieval into Listening Activities?

Repetition and spaced retrieval are important in listening because they give learners more exposure to the target vocabulary. Once learners have listened, gained meaning from the text, and worked on their vocabulary, they need to make sure that this new learning is not lost once they leave the classroom. Listening to the same material several times is a useful way to make sure that the words and their context become more firmly a part of the learners' vocabulary. I often ask my learners to listen first for understanding, second for language and thirdly for fluency.

There are many ways to build repetition and retrieval into listening activities. Here are some suggestions:

- Listen again with no stopping.
- Stop just after the target words to discuss meaning and/or use.
- Stop before the target word and ask learners to say what they recall comes next—making sure that the target words are part of the text reconstruction. You could use the target words as prompts.

For some learners, however, listening again and again will not help them because they are struggling with actually hearing words as they are spoken. For these learners, it is important that they spend time working on establishing a link between the written and spoken forms of words.

How Can We Help Learners to Recognise Academic Words When They Are Spoken?

Some learners find it difficult to match the written form of the word to the spoken form. Why might learners need help to recognize words when they are spoken?

- Some people learn mostly through listening and therefore do not have much previous experience with the written word.
- Other students have learned the language mostly through reading, in which case the spoken form can cause problems.
- Others may not be able to match the sounds they hear with the information about the words they have stored in their long-term memory.[9]

Here are some activities for matching the written and spoken forms of words.

- Give learners a copy of the text you are working on with the target words in bold or highlighted in some way. Ask learners to follow along with the text while listening, underlining the words as they hear them.
- Have learners read the passage before listening so they engage fully with the text and are very familiar with it before they start listening intensely.[10] You could ask them to read aloud, in pairs, silently or in groups.
- Have learners put target words on flash cards. As they listen, they order the cards as the words occur in the text. They can then use these cards to:
  - Listen for more detail such as collocations around the words.
  - Retell the text.
  - Test other students on different aspects of the words.
  - Place in a vocabulary box for whole-class access for further individual learning. For more on learning with flash cards, see Chapter 5.

- Write the target words on the board and have learners write them down. They then tick the words off or say them to themselves as they hear them when they listen to the passage again.
- Create dictations with the key words in them. You can deliver the dictations yourself or:
  - Students can dictate to each other, using passages they have selected from their own reading or from class.
  - They can read short sequences of a text, look away and repeat the text to a partner.
  - Learners can do running dictations with the text in another part of the room or outside.[11] I have yet to meet a class that hasn't found running dictations challenging, memorable and fun.
- Before listening, do pronunciation work on the words to activate the connection between the sounds and the words.[12]
- Read through the passage with learners, providing meanings and pronunciation examples as you go. Put the key words on the board as they come up in the passage, thereby drawing more attention to their form.[13] For example, the following text has words from the AWL in **bold**.

> There is plenty of **research** now that shows that almost anyone can learn a foreign language by **creating** a positive **environment** and following certain **strategies** for success. There are lots of ordinary people who have become fluent in foreign languages by following some basic **principles**. You require a **complex** set of skills which involve your whole self. That means your emotions, your thoughtful **processing**, and your **physical** self.[14]

As you and learners read, you could draw attention to these words by asking what they mean. You could also ask how the words sound, what words they collocate with in the text, what word family members they know and so on.

Why Is Activating Background Knowledge Important for Listening and Academic Vocabulary?

It is important to activate learners' background knowledge before they start to listen. Some students may not be able to understand what they are listening to because they lack prior knowledge or are not applying their background knowledge properly.[15]

You can help activate background knowledge by starting a class-based discussion on listening. You can also use this time with the class to gather vocabulary items the class already knows in connection with the topic. Some target words may well come up in the brainstorm, in which case you will need to gauge how well-known they are and whether learners need further teaching or learning before they hear these words in context.

With academic subject materials there is often debate—ideas on development in areas such as technology and science, or concepts on different aspects of life or discovery in human lives. Pre-listening tasks can focus on the type of topic. For example, if the listening is from a news report on the use of text messaging for bullying in schools, introduce the topic through questions that set the students talking with a critical focus to their answers. Use the target words in the input if you can, so that learners are given an opportunity to see the words and perhaps use them in their pre-listening task.[16] For example:

Text-messaging and bullying:

What are some of the advantages and disadvantages of **technological** developments such as mobile phones?

Are these advantages and disadvantages the same for everyone?

Do you think mobile phone use should be restricted in schools or should schools take a **liberal approach** to them? Why/why not?

If the materials are high-interest and learners already know a lot about the topic, then you have very good conditions for listening, providing the text does not contain too many unknown words. Talking about a topic is listening practice in its most basic form, so the activation of prior knowledge might also help scaffold or build the learners up to the more difficult listening event.

Endnotes

1. Nation, P., & P. Meara. 2002. Vocabulary. In Schmitt, N. (Ed.) *Introduction to applied linguistics.* Arnold: London. See especially page 50.
2. Vidal, K. 2003. Academic listening: a source of vocabulary acquisition? *Applied Linguistics 24*(1), 56–89.
3. Vidal, 2003.
4. Nation, P. 2001. *Learning vocabulary in another language.* Cambridge: Cambridge University Press. See especially page 121.
5. Nation, 2001. See especially page 118.
6. One way of finding out what interests your learners is to ask them to bring something they enjoy listening to into class to share with other students. You could also do a quick class survey to find out what topics they like learning about. Also ask other teachers and learners what current topics they find interesting.
7. Rost, M. 1994. *Introducing listening.* Penguin: London. See especially page 147.
8. The oral communication for academic purposes books in this Houghton Mifflin series provide a useful base to work on listening and academic vocabulary.
9. Goh, C. 2000. A cognitive perspective on language learners listening comprehension problems. *System 28,* 55–75.
10. For more suggestions on strategies and practice for improving listening comprehension, see Goh, 2000.
11. For more dictation ideas, see Davis, P., & M. Rinvolucri. 1988. *Dictations. New methods, new possibilities.* Cambridge: Cambridge University Press. For more on running dictations and other dictation ideas with academic vocabulary, see Chapter 11 in Part 3 of this book.
12. For more on pronunciation work with words in the AWL, see Murphy, J. and M. Kandil. 2004. Word-level stress patterns in the Academic Word List. *System 32,* 61–74.
13. Nation, 2001. See especially page 117.
14. Adapted from Brown, H. D. 1989. *A practical guide to language learning.* New York: McGraw-Hill. See especially page 1.
15. Goh, 2000. See especially page 59.
16. Newton, J. 1995. Task-based interaction and incidental vocabulary learning: A case study. *Second Language Research 11,* 159–177.

Chapter **11**

Academic Vocabulary in Listening Activities

FEATURED IN THIS CHAPTER

- What activities focus on academic vocabulary before listening?
- What vocabulary learning activities can you use during listening?
- What vocabulary learning activities can you use after listening?

This chapter is in three parts. We will be looking at classroom activities focussing on working closely with academic vocabulary pre-, during and post-listening. Many of these activities can be adapted for use with reading, speaking or writing.

What Activities Focus on Vocabulary Before Listening?

One major point to remember is that pre-teaching words does not automatically ensure that learners will be able to recall them after the listening, or even recognise them during the listening. It is important to make sure the words are part of a program of rich instruction. Learners need to work with them in many ways. The following are some pre-listening activities using examples from texts that students will then listen to in order to check their answers. These activities include matching, meaning checks and dictations.[1]

Matching Tasks

Matching tasks require concentration and evaluation. They can include a focus on matching meaning and form, but can be widened to also focus on collocations and word families. For example:

- Matching meanings and words. In this exercise, students match the meaning in the left column with a word from the box below.

MEANING	AWL WORD FROM BOX BELOW
need	
in law	
show	
exact	
meaning opposite of minor	

authority	occur	response	legal
create	thereby	definition	indicate
principle	specific	major	require

- Matching collocations and words. You could use this type of table or make a freer exercise like the one that follows.

Here is an example of matching common collocations to the key words. Learners find a collocation for each AWL word in the second column and then put that collocation either before or after the target word. Some collocations may fit in several places. There is a fuller version of this exercise on this book's website.

Collocation before	AWL Word	Collocation after	Collocations
			crucial
	major		health problems
			improvement
	indicate		mathematical
			of energy
	source		policy
			that something is true
	formula		to an emergency

The following matching exercise requires students to create their own collocations, as opposed to just choosing a supplied one.

Write collocations for each AWL word either BEFORE or AFTER the word. The first one is done for you:

Collocation	AWL Word	Collocation
	major	1. *investment* 2.
	create	1. 2.
1. 2.	data	
	legal	1. 2.

If you create a matching exercise based on a listening passage, learners can then listen to see whether their collocations were the ones used in the passage. You could also ask students to:

- Listen to a text and note the target phrases or longer collocations. Students could also note how sounds change when phrases are spoken naturally. These exercises could help learners identify individual words within chunks. It may help them start to distinguish words from each other rather then hearing a jumble of sounds.
- Match word family members and target words. For example:

Fill in the gaps in the word families in this table.

VERB	NOUN	ADJECTIVE
		structural
		creative
	specification	
economise		

Pre-Listening Meaning Check

You can quickly check meaning in many ways. For example:

- Put the words on the board and ask learners to discuss what they know about them.
- Practice vocabulary-learning strategies with the words before listening. For example, learners could practice the key word technique on target academic words. See Chapter 5 for more on the key word technique.
- Give brief quizzes on words and their meanings. Whether you grade these quizzes or not is up to you.

Pre-Listening Dictation

Pre-listening dictation with the key words also can be useful. Be sure that
the target vocabulary occurs in the dictation. Texts can be dictated in
several ways, including:

- Dictate from learner to learner. Learners could do this as a
  back-to-back dictation or for more action, as a running dictation,
  with the text either on the wall outside the room, or being read
  in chunks to the 'runner.'
- Be traditional and have teachers dictate to learners. You could vary
  the speed of the dictation or use a *whistle* dictation.[2]
- Dictate part by part or as a whole.

Here is an example of a dictation using a passage on conservation.
I have cut the text into short chunks at first. You will notice that the
chunks get longer as the text goes on. The first few chunks have been
marked already. How would you chunk the last sentence of this passage?

> Reduce,/ reuse and recycle/ are three important components/ related
> to the conservation/ of the environment./ They are similar ideas/ that
> contribute to clean communities./ If you reduce waste/ you avoid
> buying products/ you do not need./ This strategy can assist people and
> help them adapt their wasteful habits from the past.[3]

Here is a possible answer: *This strategy can assist people/ and help them
adapt their wasteful habits/ from the past.*

To further focus on the vocabulary in the dictation passage, you could
follow it up with activities such as:

- Having learners reconstruct the text as best they can, using the target
  words as key prompts.
- Putting the key words on the board and together checking
  spelling/meaning/word families/collocations from the text.
- Giving learners a copy of the text to check their own work. They
  could then analyze the kinds of vocabulary errors they have made
  and how they might fix that problem for the future.

What Vocabulary Learning Activities Can You Use During Listening?

Here are some ideas for activities that focus on vocabulary while learners are listening. They can be used during or after listening, or for reviewing later.

■ Using the original tape script, replace the target academic words with synonyms that are more frequent in English or that you are sure your learners know well. For example, instead of *aid* write *help*, instead of *donate* or *contribute* write *give*. Have learners replace the synonyms with the words they hear in the text. For example:

Replace each high-frequency word in italics with a synonym from the Academic Word List. Then listen to check your answers.

One of the most useful ideas about human memory is that it is the depth of what happens in our brains that *influences* how well something is remembered. To put it another way, the quantity of learning depends on the quality of mental processing at the time of learning. This *way* is more important than communication, *developing* a good learning *situation*, and having clear *aims*.[4]

Answers: affects, strategy, creating, environment, goals.

■ Insert the starting letters of key words in the tape script and have learners predict what the ends of the words will be. Then have them listen to check. For example:

Read through the following text and complete the words from the Academic Word List in the blanks. Listen to check your answers.

In the early years of settlement in New Zealand (NZ) there was a close rela_____ between Australia and NZ. The figures showing immigration to Wellington illus_____ this distinct influence. A considerable prop_____ of these people would have been speakers of a colonial var_____ of Australian English.[5]

Answers: relationship, illustrate, proportion, variety.

Sample AWL Fill-in-the-Blank on Nuclear Power

Nuclear power is the subject of a great deal of _____ in the world today. Some people argue that it is a reliable _____ to _____ sources of energy such as oil and gas. The advocates of nuclear power often comment that it is an important _____ of progress in the modern world.

alternative	debate	symbol	option
global	community	traditional	authority

If you want to make your own fill-in-the-blanks exercises, try the Academic Word List Gapmaker, designed by Sandra Haywood,[6] on the Internet. All you have to do is paste your electronic text into the web page, decide which sublists you would like to target for the exercise and the web page will design a fill-in-the-blanks activity for you. I try to make sure there are seven words or more between the gaps so that learners have some context to help them with the activity.

Here is an example of how the AWL Gapmaker website works using a paragraph from Chapter 3 of this book. If you put this paragraph into the AWL Gapmaker website and request that the words from the AWL Sublist 1 are taken out, your text will look like this:

Fill-in-the-blank passage with AWL words highlighted from Sublists 1–10 of the AWL.

The [   ] of frequency, repetition and spaced retrieval from [   ] one and two are clearly represented in this [   ]. This is because they are key to the [   ] of words becoming part of what we call our [   ] 'lexicon' or our own [   ] dictionaries. Another important point is that learners need to be actively [   ] in this [   ] and to understand each part. In other words, learners need to know how and why they are learning these words.

The following words will fill the gaps:

chapters	internal	involved	mental	principles	process	process	process

- You can widen the scope of the fill-in-the-blank exercises by requiring learners to fill in chunks of language or phrases. This means they need to listen for the target vocabulary and the collocations that occur with these words.

What Vocabulary Learning Activities Can You Use After Listening?

Activities after listening based on the words and expressions coming from the text are an important part of the learning process for two main reasons. First, the repetition and retrieval needed for learning is built into the task. Second, there is opportunity for learners to test out the words or check their understanding of them. Here is a sample of possible post-listening activities:

- Listening again to the same text with a focus on listening for fluency.[7]
- Listening to an extended version of the same text.
- Listening to a wider range of contexts with similar topics.
- Retelling the text either with or without the source text for support.[8]
- Creating discussions, role plays or debates based on scenarios from a passage learners have used in class. Be sure to include the target vocabulary in the preparation for the discussion. For example, a listening activity on conserving endangered species in New Zealand from a radio program on the Kiwi, a flightless native bird, could form the basis for further speaking and therefore listening practice on a topic such as:

> The government should invest more money in conserving endangered species in New Zealand.[9]

See Chapter 12 for more ideas on vocabulary-focussed speaking activities.

- Conducting quizzes based on the vocabulary in the text. Quizzes do not always have to be an assessment tool. They also can be used to trigger recall of vocabulary and provide learners with another encounter with a word.

You can encourage learners to get a good return for learning effort while doing these activities by getting them to:

- Prepare well for these tasks.
- See that they are challenged to use the vocabulary fluently and accurately.
- Be clear about the learning outcome of the activity.
- Operate with some sort of time pressure.

Allow for some review time between activities so students can reflect on their use of the vocabulary, correct some errors and improve their next performance.

Endnotes

1. Full versions of these activity sheets are on this book's website at http://www.college.hmco.com/esl/instructors.
2. See this book's website for instructions on how to do a running dictation or a whistling dictation.
3. Adapted from *The Canadian green consumer guide.* 1989. The Pollution Probe Foundation. Toronto: McClelland & Stewart Inc.
4. Based on an abstract from Paul Nation, 31 July 2003. Levels of processing hypothesis. Lecture at Victoria University of Wellington, New Zealand
5. Adapted from Gordon, E., & T. Deverson. 1985. *New Zealand English.* Auckland: Heinemann.
6. The Academic Word List Gapmaker by Sandra Haywood is available at http://www.nottingham.ac.uk/~alzsh3/acvocab/awlgapmaker.htm.
7. Listening for fluency involves similar conditions as reading for fluency. The listening material should not have too many unknown words and the passage should be familiar to learners already. For more on fluency and vocabulary, see Nation, P. 2001. *Learning vocabulary in another language.* Cambridge: Cambridge.
8. Simcock, M. 1993. Developing productive vocabulary using the 'Ask and answer' technique. *Guidelines 15*, 1–7.
9. I based this idea on readings from a study theme from Victoria University of Wellington.

Chapter 12

Speaking and Academic Vocabulary

FEATURED IN THIS CHAPTER

- What speaking task features can be used to encourage academic vocabulary learning?
- What aspects of academic vocabulary are important for speaking?

Learning vocabulary through speaking is a cyclical activity. While learners are speaking, they are using words in a creative way. This is a complex task, especially when learners are attempting to use academic vocabulary accurately and fluently.[1] We know that an academic language focus requires learners to perform academic tasks. So in this chapter we will be looking at speaking task features that are important to learning vocabulary and aspects of academic words that are important for producing them in speaking.

What Features of Speaking Tasks Can Be Used to Encourage Academic Vocabulary Learning?

We know that learners have to read and listen to academic texts to gain substantial exposure to academic vocabulary.[2] Therefore learners must speak and write about academic topics to produce academic language. Topics such as pets, holidays and festivals do not tend to provide many opportunities for students to generate academic vocabulary such as *analysis*, *ongoing*, and *facilitation*. Therefore a main feature of speaking tasks for developing academic vocabulary is that the context needs to be academic in nature.

Nation[3] lists four ways to make sure vocabulary is central to speaking. These relate to all vocabulary learning, but we will be looking at them in terms of academic vocabulary development.

1. The target words need to be included in any text used. It is also important that the words are salient because learners tend not to negotiate words that are not directly concerned with the task. Teachers need to think about the instructions for tasks to ensure that they include the target vocabulary. Lots of written input for speaking tasks is also important. If the speaking activity follows a reading task, for example, then make sure you exploit the written material as much as possible for the speaking task.

2. Make sure the written input is necessary to do the speaking task. You can do this by basing the tasks on the text. For example, in a role play based on a reading about genetically-modified foods, you can base the speaking parts on key people in the original text, rather than on what learners themselves think.

3. Learners need to participate in the activity. For example, in role plays, assign a role to each learner and make clear they are expected to participate. You can change the roles to keep interest high.

4. Make sure the task fosters vocabulary development. Also make sure learners are aware that part of their language task is to use newly learned words in their speaking. Tell them that using the words is an important part of the learning process. Here are some suggestions to ensure the vocabulary is being used in activities:

- Encourage students to attempt to use the words in a new context.

- Have the learner tick words off a list as they use them or have other students listen and tick the words off.
- Record and play back to see if the words were used or whether there were missed opportunities for using them.
- Give learners a chance to work together and help each other recognise and fill in gaps.[4]
- Use quizzes and games that encourage learners to put words into sentences in speaking. For example, you could have regular games of matching words and their common collocations and then put them into a sentence or include them in a discussion.

What Aspects of Academic Vocabulary Are Important for Speaking?

Learners need to know many words well in order to take part in conversations.[5] Speaking is clearly different from listening and reading since learners need to use or produce academic vocabulary to demonstrate that they know the words. To use the words well, learners must have fluency and accuracy. We will look first at these two aspects of speaking, and then move on to meaning, pronunciation and levels of formality.

Fluency

Developing fluency in vocabulary use is important in speaking and is an important step towards knowing a word. Fluency involves using the vocabulary you already know.[6] It also includes maintaining the vocabulary by using it regularly and correctly, and attending to feedback. Repetition is an enormous aid to fluency because repetition gives learners the chance to use the words over again within a short amount of time. Here are some ways to build repetition into tasks for fluency practice:

- Set up activities for fluency clearly so that learners are well aware that fluency is the purpose.
- Give speakers a new audience each time they repeat a speaking activity.
- Increase the time pressure on the repeat performance. This may result in fewer hesitations while speaking.
- Impose test or performance conditions within reason. A little extra pressure while speaking may help with fluency development.

- Repeat the task with a time lapse of a day or two.
- Change the task slightly. For example, if learners have been role playing, have them instead participate in a mock television programme. Learners could present their discussion to the class as a television debate, news report, or reality program. Learners could be rated on their fluency and accuracy in using the target vocabulary in their television reports.

While fluency in speaking is an important goal in vocabulary development, students also need to become accurate in their use of academic vocabulary.

Accuracy

Accuracy in using academic vocabulary has several aspects. Accuracy can include meaning, pronunciation, collocations and levels of formality. For students who are reluctant to use words for fear of inaccuracy or lack of knowledge, teachers need to provide support. This can be done by:

- Allowing students to use planning time to prepare well for tasks.
- Establishing clear aims in the activity.
- Giving learners rehearsal time before any 'performance.'
- Making sure the feedback on speaking encourages learners to look at their language and to make adjustments.
- Providing time for further practice to make good use of the feedback.

Meaning

Learners gradually develop a picture of each word based on previous encounters with it. Each new meeting supports or adds to the previous learning. Repetition and spaced retrieval are important principles to keep in mind. Too much time between encounters leads quickly to forgetting. See Chapter 4 for teaching a word's core meaning and explaining word meanings. See Chapters 7 and 10 for more ideas on teaching meaning.

Pronunciation

Some learners may find it difficult to pronounce long academic words. For example, the word *environment* can take a bit of effort to say it with the correct pronunciation and stress.

Here are a couple of techniques for working on pronunciation:

- Encourage learners to learn a word's pronunciation as part of their word-attack strategy. They could focus on word stress as well as the overall sound of the word.
- Break the words into smaller units of sound and get learners to back chain them like this:

  -tion, ation, cation, munication, communication.

  You could then work these words into sentences for practice.
- Teach the phonetic alphabet used in dictionaries. This can help learners both in and out of class. Once they have mastered the basics of the phonetic alphabet, they are better equipped to get pronunciation information from a dictionary.
- Present regular rules of stress,[7] for example, words ending with *-ation* are stressed on the syllable before the suffix or final part of the word.
- Try review activities such as asking learners to group words from a list or table into ones with the same stress pattern, or ones with the same number of syllables. For example, arrange the following words according to their stress patterns.

behalf	justify	eliminate	widespread	create
incentive	somewhat	locate	virtual	equate

- Record learners using the words and provide practice and feedback on their individual pronunciations.
- Have regular pronunciation checks on key words. For example, you can write key words on the board and elicit their pronunciation.

- Have several pronunciation drills up your sleeve for practice. For example:
    - Check that learners can hear the correct word stress by saying the word several times with correct or incorrect stress and asking them which was correct. Once they consistently get the right answer, have learners do the same in pairs.[8]
    - Put the key words on the board and as you point to each, have learners, alone, in pairs or as a group, say them in different ways (e.g., softly, loudly, in a whisper, angrily).
    - Explain how to backchain sentences to focus on the word stress in sentences. To backchain, start with the end of the sentence and ask students to repeat the last word, then say the last two words and repeat, then the last three words and so on. For example, here is the sentence:

This is how you backchain.

The backchain goes:

backchain
you backchain
how you backchain
is how you backchain
This is how you backchain.

A useful technique for learners who really do find a word impossible to say is to replace the word with a synonym and avoid saying the word if possible.

Levels of Formality

Learners need to be aware of whether they are using appropriate vocabulary for academic tasks. In Chapter 8, we saw how the words that occur in a section of *The Jungle Book* are very different from those in an academic text on accounting. For some learners it may be a surprise that in some ways, the words you use in speaking about academic topics are different from those in your everyday language.

You could model formal speaking and vocabulary use by examining example sentences with learners in terms of what kinds of words occur in everyday language. Common greetings can be a good example to look at.

In New Zealand, we have a number of ways of greeting people. We might, for example:

- Say *kia ora* in Maori, the indigenous language of New Zealand.
- Make eye contact with the other person, lift our eyebrows slightly in acknowledgment and say nothing.
- Use the short form of *good day* and say *gidday.*[9]
- Greet the person with *good morning.*

How we greet someone depends on our relationship with the person. A change in audience leads to a change of greeting. You could demonstrate this by asking learners which greeting they would use with an old friend from primary school, their parents, the Queen of England, the President of the United States, or their teacher.

You could move the conversation on to vocabulary in academic speaking and to how the level of formality rises. Model upgrading the formality of sentences (within reason) to ensure that academic vocabulary is brought forward in learners' minds to be used when they are explaining complex ideas in speaking.

Endnotes

1. See *Essentials of teaching academic oral communication* by John Murphy and *College Oral Communication* textbooks in this Houghton Mifflin series for more suggestions and exercises on vocabulary in speaking.
2. Coxhead, A. 2000. A new academic word list, *TESOL Quarterly, 34*(2), 213–238.
3. Nation, P. 2001. *Learning vocabulary in another language.* Cambridge: Cambridge University Press. See especially page 140.
4. Joe, A., P. Nation, & J. Newton. 1996. Vocabulary learning and speaking activities. *English Teaching Forum.* 34, pp. 2–7.
5. Adolphs, S., & N. Schmitt. 2003. Lexical coverage of spoken discourse, *Applied linguistics 24*(4), 425–438.
6. Nation, 2001. See especially page 337.
7. For more ideas on teaching word stress, see Murphy, J. 2004. Attending to word stress while learning new vocabulary, *Journal of English for Specific Purposes, 23,* 67–83 and Murphy, J. 2004. Word level stress in EAP oral communication. *Houghton Mifflin ESL/ELT academic success newsletter,* 2: 1–3.
8. I learned this technique from Paul Nation, Victoria University of Wellington.
9. Of course, you would use the pronunciation appropriate to the English your students are learning!

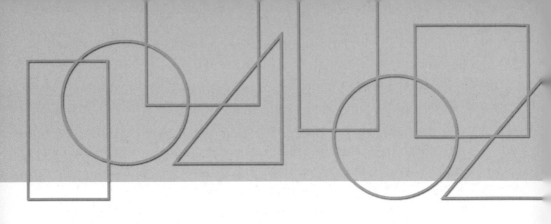

Chapter 13

Academic Vocabulary in Speaking Activities

FEATURED IN THIS CHAPTER

- What speaking activities can we use for vocabulary learning?
- How can we give feedback on academic vocabulary used in speaking?

In this chapter we will be looking at classroom activities that are focussed on using academic vocabulary in speaking, including formal speaking, role playing and discussions. We will also look at giving feedback on vocabulary use in speaking.

What Speaking Activities Can We Use for Vocabulary Learning?

For any speaking task focussed on developing academic vocabulary, you need to first ensure that the discussion topics are academic in nature.

The topics need to require learners to stretch themselves in some way. You can turn almost any topic into a more academic style simply by asking learners to:

- Compare and contrast two aspects of a topic. For example, *compare learning your first language with learning your second language.* You might consider your learning **environment**, your **awareness** of learning processes and your learning **strategies**.
- State disadvantages and advantages. For example, *do the advantages of living in this century outweigh the disadvantages?*
- Justify why something is the case. For example, *why should there be a 'no drugs' policy in secondary schools?*
- Give the plus, minus and interesting points of a topic. For example, *explain why you think learning vocabulary in another language is not the same as learning words in your first language.*
- Explain a concept or argue a point from another point of view. For example, *write a report for a company on the viability of introducing a genetically engineered food product into supermarkets in New Zealand.*[1]
- Describe a process and explain the difficulties arising from the process, or outline a problem, stating the causes and providing and evaluating solutions to the problem. For example, *outline the problems caused by the hole in the ozone layer. What is the best solution to this environmental problem? Provide evidence and examples to support your opinions.*

Ask learners to select academic words they want to focus on in the activity so they realise vocabulary development is a major goal of the task.

Here are some classroom activities that you might like to try to encourage vocabulary use in speaking. One useful technique with any of these activities is to record native or near-native speakers performing these tasks for learners to observe and analyze. The emphasis here is on developing noticing skills and encouraging learners to start using their ears to recognize and understand academic vocabulary.

- In the **4-3-2**[2] activity, learners prepare a short talk (with vocabulary input and an academic topic). They speak for 4 minutes, then 3 minutes, and finally 2 minutes with different listeners. The

4-3-2 activity builds fluency because learners make fewer errors in their later attempts with a shorter amount of time. Here are some key points about the 4-3-2 activity:

- The pressure of time commits the students to making key points quickly while maintaining their focus on the message.
- With a little inbuilt revision time between talks, learners can substantially improve their fluency and raise the level of language they are using.
- Students need to be aware of the importance of repeating activities in order to build fluency.
- For variation, at the end of each speaking time have the listener ask a question. This adds focus for the listener and provides speakers with a little more speaking time. It also helps provide speakers with some feedback for revising the content or language of their talks.

- In **pyramid discussions**,[3] learners rank a list of items and then discuss their ranking with a partner in order for them to rank the items again. Each pair then meets up with another pair and tries to rank the items so that all agree. The ranked items should contain academic vocabulary so that learners are exposed to the words and are encouraged as much as possible to use them when they are speaking. Here is an example of a pyramid discussion; AWL words are in **bold**:

Which of the following factors do you think are crucial to language learning and why? Select your top three and then discuss your opinions with a partner. Try to agree with your partner on a top three list.

A high level of **analytical** ability.
A positive **attitude** towards language learning.
A desire to **communicate** with people from other cultures.
A highly **innovative** teacher.
Cutting-edge **technology**.
Setting **realistic** goals.
Creating opportunities to use the target language.
Using a wide **variety** of **strategies**.

- **Retelling**[4] involves reading and then retelling the main ideas of what you have read. This activity provides new vocabulary and a context for understanding the new words. Taking the text away during speaking leads to more generation of vocabulary but keeping the text during retelling means more vocabulary is used.[5]
- **Role playing** based on class input can encourage vocabulary use. Students can prepare their roles first and then take part in a debate or discussion to help vocabulary fluency. For example, if the topic is that *Canada should become part of the United States,* learners could take one of the following roles:

> **You are the Prime Minister of Canada. Do you agree or disagree with integrating your country with the United States? What economic, social and political arguments can you put forward to support your point of view? What other arguments can you use in the upcoming discussion?**

> **You are the President of the United States. Do you agree or disagree with Canada integrating with your country? What economic, social and political arguments can you put forward to support your point of view? What other arguments can you use in the upcoming discussion?**

Other roles that could be added as examples are leaders of nearby countries who may or may not want Canada to become part of the United States, U.S. and Canadian citizens representing the voice of regular people, or business people in each country.[6]

- **Impromptu speaking** involves preparing a short talk, preferably on an academic topic. As part of the preparation, learners could choose 15 words from the Academic Word List to use in their talk. Give learners time to prepare and rehearse before they present their talk to the class.
- **Debates** on academic topics can foster vocabulary generation. As learners prepare, they can select academic words to use. Learners can take opposing sides of the topic and discuss it in groups. Reading and listening tasks (especially from current events) can often provide good debate material.

- **Ping-Pong discussions** in which learners debate the pros and cons of a proposition can include the added challenge of ensuring that they use a certain number of target words when speaking.
- **Making your own news broadcasts**[7] involves reading about recent news events and then creating a radio or television news broadcast in the class.
- **Poster carousel**[8] sessions involve learners reading a text such as a journal article, newspaper story or chapter from a text book and preparing a poster based on what they have read. Split the class into half or thirds and have part of the class display their posters while the others move around and listen to the discussion of each poster and ask questions about the content. The repetition in this activity effectively builds fluency.
- **Surveys, interviews and round table discussions** can encourage learners to use vocabulary in speaking.
- **Preparing a presentation or seminar** whereby learners can plan the words they will use, rehearse the talks and present them to the class with time allowed for questions.

Learners need to be fully aware that a main purposes of the activity is to use the target words appropriately and fluently to gain mastery of them in their speaking.

Finally, remember that learners need opportunities to express their ideas using the vocabulary in ways that are relevant to themselves.[9] Students could continue an academic debate by seeking out opportunities to discuss ideas with students outside class.

How Can We Give Feedback on Vocabulary Used in Speaking?

One of the key elements of using vocabulary in speaking is to get feedback on its use. Feedback can be given on different aspects of a word. Meaning is another key element simply because using words out of context and incorrectly means learners may not be understood when they speak. Collocations, word families, grammatical errors and pronunciation problems can also be part of the feedback to speakers, depending on the type of error. It is important to remember that the errors that stand in the way of understanding need to be focussed on early. Speaking events such as seminars can be recorded so students can use the tape for self-analysis or feedback on their vocabulary.

Teachers can spend a great deal of time giving feedback on writing and speaking. In terms of focussing on academic vocabulary, there are several key questions to keep in mind with feedback:

- What is the nature of the error? There are times when pronunciation errors are closely linked with grammatical errors. For example, if a student misses the plural '*s*' when they say 'There are two strategy.' Is this an error in grammar, vocabulary knowledge or pronunciation?
- What is the purpose of the feedback? Is it to point out the errors only, to raise the students' awareness of areas to focus on, or to develop and challenge the students' use of academic vocabulary?
- How persistent is the error? Does it occur regularly or systematically or does it happen rarely?
- Does the error impede communication? If the errors mean that the student cannot be understood by the listener, then there is clearly work to be done immediately.
- Is the problem a matter of style or register? Sometimes a learner is largely correct when they use a word but if the formality level is wrong, then they are making a judgment error on the correctness of language for a particular situation.
- Would the student benefit more from error correction at the time of the error or later? In connection with this point is the problem of how much attention to give an error.

It may be worthwhile to ask students to rank the errors they need to work on first. This sort of discussion can further raise student awareness of lexical difficulties. Also useful could be a discussion on what strategies students could employ to correct these errors. Finally, ensure there is an opportunity to work on the speaking again and to present an improved version later in class.

Teachers need to make clear from the start that the feedback will focus on the use of vocabulary during the task.[10] Learners also need to understand that it is feedback when it is being given.

- Avoid echoing the incorrect word as students may take the echo as confirmation that you are listening, rather than attempting a correction.

- Decide together when the speaking corrections will take place.[11] If an activity is purely focussed on fluency, perhaps you and the students could agree that instead of interrupting them as they speak, you will:
  - Take note of any significant errors and do some error correction as a class at the end of the activity.
  - Give feedback either spoken or written directly to individual students.
- Talk about what to do with feedback once it has been signalled. Learners might decide to stop and try again, or note the feedback for the next time they use the target vocabulary.
- Take notes as you listen to your learners trying to use the vocabulary and conduct a feedback session on common errors for the class.
- Have learners repeat their speaking activity after they have received feedback and have had time to process and correct the errors on their vocabulary use. The repetition of the activity is useful for fluency and learners are also concentrating on getting the use of the words right.
- Reformulate the task slightly to add interest and encourage repetition. You can do this by changing the audience, setting a speaking time limit or getting the students to aim for a higher accuracy level when speaking.

At the end of the activity, learners may also try to mentally note the correction and make a written note of the feedback if they need to. Once you decide on the feedback, what will you want the learners to do with it? You could perhaps:

- Test learners directly using quizzes based on the key points in the vocabulary-based feedback. For example, depending on the nature of the errors your students are making, you could ask learners to:
  - Correct errors in meaning or use in sentences.
  - Supply the correct collocation for words.
  - Work on the pronunciation.
  - Name the parts of speech for the word family members.
  - Use the words correctly in sentences.
- Have learners create an *error journal*[12] where they record the sentence with the original error, the correction of the error and whether they consider that error important. Error journals can help learners prepare for speaking by reminding them of errors they wish to avoid with their target vocabulary.

Endnotes

1. I got this topic from an academic writing programme at Massey University, Palmerston North, New Zealand.
2. Maurice, K. 1983. The fluency workshop, *TESOL Newsletter,* 8.
3. Jordan, R. 1990. Pyramid discussions. *ELTJ, 44*(1), 46–54.
4. Joe, A., P. Nation & J. Newton. 1996. Vocabulary learning and speaking activities. *English Teaching Forum. 34,* 2–7.
5. Joe, A. 1994. The effect of text-based tasks on incidental vocabulary learning. Unpublished MA thesis. Wellington: Victoria University of Wellington.
6. For more suggestions on using role play in language classrooms, see Di Pietro. 1987. *Strategic interaction.* Cambridge: Cambridge University Press and Ladousse, G. 1987. *Role play.* Oxford: Oxford University Press.
7. Coxhead, A. 1997. 'Radio news' and 'Making our own news.' In M. Lewis (Ed.), *New Ways in Teaching Adults,* (pp. 4–8). TESOL: Alexandra, VA.
8. Lynch, T., & J. McLean. 2000. Exploring the benefits of task repetition and recycling for classroom language learning. *Language Teaching Research,* 1 September 2000, vol. 4, no. 3, pp. 221–250.
9. Thornbury, S. 2002. *How to teach vocabulary.* Longman: Harlow, Essex.
10. Ellis, R., H. Basturkmen & S. Loewen. 2002. Doing focus on form. *System, 30*(4), 419–432.
11. I first learned of this technique from Sara Cotterall, Victoria University of Wellington, New Zealand.
12. I first learned of *error journals* from the English Language Institute, Victoria University of Wellington, New Zealand.

Chapter **14**

Writing and Academic Vocabulary

FEATURED IN THIS CHAPTER

- How can we develop academic vocabulary through writing?
- What do you need to keep in mind about academic vocabulary and writing?
- What aspects of vocabulary are important for writing?

One of the major problems with writing and vocabulary for learners is they tend to rely on a small number of words or a basic vocabulary.[1] In this chapter, we will look at ways to help learners use academic vocabulary in their writing.

How Can We Learn Academic Vocabulary Through Writing?

Using new words in writing is very important for helping establish the meaning and use of words in learners' memories. Learners are more likely to remember a word's meaning if it is used productively in a vocabulary-focussed task than if they just come across it in a reading text.[2]

Learners need reinforcement in vocabulary use in writing. In a small-scale study of vocabulary use in student writing, Lee[3] found that learners increased their production of target words after direct vocabulary instruction, but the learning was not retained over the long term. Here are ways to include the principles of frequency, repetition, spaced retrieval, and generation of academic vocabulary in writing activities:

- **Frequency**—to examine your students' writing to find out what proportion of high-frequency, academic and other words they are using in their writing, you can use the Range Programme with your students' texts.[4] On Tom Cobb's website,[5] you can enter your students' texts for an analysis of the vocabulary frequency. Your students might like to see their lexical results as part of building awareness of their academic vocabulary use.
- **Repetition**—use recycling activities that focus on learners using target words again after they received feedback on their use of the words.
- **Spaced retrieval**—develop vocabulary-focussed activities as part of the writing process to encourage vocabulary use. You could work on activities such as brainstorming, vocabulary mind-maps and developing skills in using reference texts such as a thesaurus.[6]
- **Generation**—encourage learners to use academic words in new contexts in their writing.

What Do You Need to Keep in Mind About Academic Vocabulary and Writing?

Writing about academic topics is important for academic writing. If we look at the following two topics, which one do you think would encourage the use of academic words such as *widespread, reject, inevitable, innovation* and *manipulate*?

1. 'My last holiday'
2. 'What are the advantages and disadvantages of genetically-modified foods?'

It might depend on the kind of holiday you had, but I would suggest the second topic lends itself to more complex vocabulary. Selecting topics that are relevant to the writers leads to more sophisticated vocabulary.[7]

Here are some more key ideas on developing academic vocabulary through writing.

- Stress to limited users of vocabulary the need to increase their vocabulary.[8]
- My research found that on average 10 percent of an academic text is made up of words from the AWL.[9] This includes words such as *justify, assess, impact, comment, contrast, highlight* and *research.* This finding tells us that learners need to be able to recognize these words in reading and to use them in academic writing.
- It is important to have a reason for writing. Let your students know that writing gives them a chance to use words they partially know to increase their confidence in using these words.
- Help your students get information from dictionaries on academic vocabulary. Dictionaries are useful tools for writers, especially if they have the skills to find, analyze and apply knowledge about words. See Chapter 7 for more ideas on developing vocabulary and dictionaries.
- Emphasize that one meeting or use of a target word is not enough. Learners need more than that for learning. Each encounter with a word increases the learners' knowledge of that word.
- Writing on similar topics and redrafting will ensure that learners have plenty of opportunity to use target words. For example, your students might need to write an essay on a topic that they need to research.
  - Supply students with some background reading and focus on the academic vocabulary in context.
  - Set up an essay writing task whereby the essay they write uses a number of the target words.
  - Ask learners to write a report on the same topic but with a slightly different focus.[10]
- Use pre-writing activities to start learners thinking about their writing. Ensure target words are included in any pre-writing activity. Here are some pre-writing ideas that encourage learners to focus on vocabulary and writing.
  - Brainstorm ideas and vocabulary before writing. Use what learners say to construct semantic maps for learners to work from in their writing.[11]
  - Have learners choose target vocabulary they will attempt to use in their writing.

- Use speaking tasks before vocabulary tasks to promote vocabulary use. See Chapter 13 for ideas on using academic vocabulary in speaking.

What Aspects of Vocabulary Are Important for Writing?

Accuracy and fluency are important for vocabulary use in writing. Like speaking, writing is a productive skill that requires a good knowledge of many aspects of words. Here are some vocabulary aspects important for writing.

Meaning

Having the correct meaning can be very difficult when learners are using words they do not know well. Some learners may be unsure of how to use academic words well in their writing. Encourage these learners to 'read like a writer.' They can do this by:

- Looking closely at how other writers use academic vocabulary and expressions in their writing. This does not mean copying texts, but looking at expressions that are used often to see how writers use them.
- Exploring patterns of use in a controlled way. You could use class time to analyze examples of written academic language in concordances. A concordance is a list of sentences from a corpus or body of texts that provides examples of a word you examine closely.

The following is an abbreviated example of a concordance of the word *theoretically* using WordSmith[12] and a body of written academic texts. In the interest of space, I have limited the context. Look at the five occurrences of the word *theoretically* in bold. What patterns can you see in the data?

1. Hamada (1972) demonstrates ***theoretically*** that the equity
2. rush of current is very high; ***theoretically*** infinite but
3. described in Module 3 to discuss this case ***theoretically***.
4. ***Theoretically***, the current never does
5. we develop a rule that is useful ***theoretically*** and also

You might notice, for example, that *theoretically* is used in example 4 to start a sentence. You may also see that you can *discuss* or *demonstrate* something *theoretically*, and that something can be *theoretically possible*. Students could compare the use of words in the concordances with their own work.[13]

- Using matching activities with texts whereby learners try to find academic words equivalent to high-frequency items to use in their writing. For example, *help* is a frequently used word with a synonym of *aid* in the AWL. Learners need to pay careful attention to the grammatical constraints associated with each of the synonyms, however. That is, some words will not just slot neatly into a text in place of another.
- Reworking texts using academic words. A word of caution is needed here. Learners sometimes go to extremes and pile large numbers of academic words into texts ending up with a text lacking meaning or sense. Remember that my study showed AWL words on average covered 10 percent of a collection of written academic texts.[14]
- Developing good dictionary skills through practice activities in class. Learners need to be able to look up words in dictionaries and study the information on different aspects of word use. They then need to be able to transfer that knowledge into their own use of the target word in writing. These complex skills take time, patience and modeling to develop well.[15] There are some 'productive' dictionaries available now that focus on learners using the entries for words as guides for selecting the right word to use.

Fostering Variety in the Use of Vocabulary in Writing

You can help your students expand their written vocabularies by using some of the following approaches:

- Encourage learners to read as writers and find synonyms for target words in texts. They can then try to model the same variety of use in their own writing.
- Suggest AWL synonyms for students to reformulate sentences.[16] For example:
  'We looked carefully at the results to see if there was a pattern.'
  (analyze) _____.

Accuracy of Vocabulary Use

- Grammar dictations[17] or dictogloss activities whereby learners use their memories to reconstruct a text they have heard as a dictation. The task is to try to accurately recreate the meaning and information of the dictated text without necessarily using the same language.
- Error analysis whereby you give an example of a vocabulary error with an aspect of word knowledge such as collocations or word families. Have learners develop their editing skills and vocabulary knowledge by finding the errors and correcting them. Don't focus on all errors, but on errors that interfere with communication and errors that are very frequent.[18]

Spelling

Many academic words are quite long. Think about words like *approximately*, *discrimination*, *qualitative*, and *infrastructure*. There is a lot more to remember about spelling these words than words such as *home*, *walk* and *like*. Retrieval is an important part of learning to spell. Doing a little bit often is an easy way to approach the problem, rather than trying to tackle a large number of words at the same time.

Learners should avoid trying to learn how to spell words that look very similar at the same time because they risk getting the words confused.[19] See Chapter 15 for some techniques for teaching spelling of academic words.

Endnotes

1. Schmitt, N. 2000. *Vocabulary in language teaching*. Cambridge: Cambridge University Press. See especially page 155.

2. Laufer, B. 2002. Vocabulary acquisition in a second language: Do learners really acquire most vocabulary by reading? Some empirical evidence. *The Canadian Modern Language Review 59* (4), 567–587. See especially page 581.

3. Lee, S. 2003. ESL learners' vocabulary use in writing and the effects of vocabulary instruction. *System, 31*, 537–561. See especially page 550.

4. For programmes available on Paul Nation's website that can be used on any PC with Windows, see the website for this book at http://www.college.hmco.com/esl/students

5. Tom Cobb's website is available through a link on this book's website at http://www.college.hmco.com/esl/students

6. Muncie, J. 2004. Process writing and vocabulary development: comparing Lexical Frequency Profiles across drafts. *System 30*, 225–235. See especially page 234.

7. Lee, 2003. See especially page 551.

8. Schmitt, N. 2000. *Vocabulary in language teaching*. Cambridge: Cambridge University Press. See especially page 155.

9. Coxhead, A. 2000. A new academic word list *TESOL Quarterly, 34* (2), 213–238.

10. I first heard of this idea at Massey University, Palmerston North, New Zealand.

11. Nation, P. 2001. *Learning vocabulary in another language*. Cambridge: Cambridge University Press. See especially page 183.

12. Wordsmith Tools is a concordancing program available through Oxford University Press. See the website for this book for a link to the Wordsmith Tools website.

13. For more on concordances, see Nation, P. 2001. *Learning vocabulary in another language*. Cambridge: Cambridge University Press. Pages 111–112.

14. Coxhead, 2000.

15. Dictionaries can supply a great deal of useful information on vocabulary. As well as meanings, they contain details on pronunciation, word families, examples of words in use, synonyms (words that have similar meanings) and grammar.

16. Nation, 2001.

17. Wajnrub, R. 1990. *Grammar dictation*. Oxford: Oxford University Press.

18. Jordan, R. 1997. *English for academic purposes*. Cambridge: Cambridge University Press. Page 173.

19. Nation, P. 2000. Learning vocabulary in lexical sets: Dangers and guidelines. *TESOL Journal 9*, 2: 6–10.

Chapter 15

Academic Vocabulary Writing Activities

- How can we help learners recognise the written form of academic words?
- What writing activities can we use to foster academic vocabulary development?
- How can we give feedback on vocabulary used in writing?

This chapter focusses on classroom activities that foster the use of academic vocabulary in writing. We will look at helping learners to match the written form of words to the spoken form, as 'ear' learners often struggle to write the words they hear.[1] We will then move to academic writing activities and using feedback to focus on academic vocabulary development.

How Can We Help Learners Recognise the Written Form of Academic Words?

Here are some suggestions for recognising the written form of a word.

- Direct teaching of spelling with rules, word parts and patterns. Try to draw connections between the patterns of the words learners know well and the new word. For example, for learning *exemplify*, learners could make connections with the words *specify*, *identify*, *clarify* and *modify*. The noun form of these words all end in *-ication*.
- Focus with your class on the spelling of new words or word family members.
- Have students write the word. They then cover it and write it again without looking at the original.[2]
- Help learners develop their own word lists and programs as part of their independent learning.
- Use word cards with the target word written on one side. Have learners turn over the card and try to retrieve the spelling from memory.
- Teach dictionary skills so learners know how to look up words for spelling purposes.
- Complete cloze exercises whereby learners complete words with letters missing. Examples of cloze exercises follow, using the sentence, 'Here is an example of a cloze exercise:'

    Here is an ex_____ of a cloze ex____se.

    or

    Here is an _____ple of a cloze exe_____.

- Use games such as hangman and crosswords whereby learners are focussed on the written form of words.[3]

What Writing Activities Can We Use for Academic Vocabulary Development?

An important point to remember about using academic words is that learners should be writing about academic topics. In other words, writing on a topic such as 'Compare and contrast learning a first language with learning a second language' should encourage learners to use more academic words than writing on a topic such as 'Describe your house.' You could use these other prompts, as well as compare and contrast, to increase the level of thinking required to complete the task:

- Stating advantages and disadvantages.
- Evaluating ideas, concepts or arguments.
- Ranking ideas in order of importance.
- Arguing from different points of view.
- Analyzing an idea or trend.

Here are some classroom activities for working on academic vocabulary. They can all be adapted to writing on different topics depending on your classroom focus. The activities start with smaller tasks using specific words to more large-scale writing tasks involving more vocabulary.

- **Constructing sentences** using target words. For example:

    Write a sentence using the word *establish*.

- **Writing paragraphs** on academic topics using target words. Ensure your students are writing about academic topics and are focussed on using words (and contexts) they have been working on in class. For example:

  Write a paragraph on ONE of the following topics using five (5) of the words in the box. You may need to change the part of speech of the words you are using.
  learning vocabulary   current events (the news)

technology	reality	analyze	community	evolve
conflict	quantity	aid	transform	graphic

- **Creating information transfer activities** where learners fill in a table or construct a diagram using a source text.[4] You could further guide their note taking by inserting several guiding questions into the grid to focus their attention on key concepts and vocabulary.
- **Doing paraphrasing tasks.** Students can practice study skills such as paraphrasing academic texts to encourage the use of target words.[5] Learners need to closely examine the words so they can paraphrase well. In the example here, the target replacements are in **bold**.

*A scheme **was put in place** to **help** people save more **money** for their later years.*

(implement, aid, fund)

An answer might be: *The plan was **implemented** to **aid** people in putting aside **funds** for their retirement.*

- **Preparing a poster carousel.** Chapter 13 outlines poster carousels as a speaking activity but it also requires students to read and write to prepare their posters.
- **Researching and writing academic essays and reports.** By reading and researching an academic topic for an academic essay or report, learners will gain exposure to academic vocabulary. In an academic writing task, learners need to know they are expected to include some of the target academic vocabulary they have encountered in their reading.

- **Writing a newspaper article** or creating a class newspaper may encourage learners to use their academic vocabulary.
- **Creating a web page** focussed on academic vocabulary with articles, games, concordances, essays, and reports created in class may also help the learners concentrate on using academic words in their writing.
- **Writing from graphs and tables** is an important academic task that can exploit a good variety of academic vocabulary as learners describe and account for the statistics. You could use other graphics such as diagrams of processes and pie graphs as input for writing. See the website for this book for an example.

How Can We Give Feedback on Vocabulary Used in Writing?

Feedback is a vital part of the language-learning cycle. While feedback can provide a wealth of language input for individual learners, it can also be handled effectively so all learners can benefit. See Chapter 13 for ideas on giving feedback on spoken language. You might be able to adapt some of those ideas for use with written language.

Here are some key ideas about giving feedback on your learners' use of target vocabulary in their writing:

- Let students know that you will be looking closely at their vocabulary use for the purpose of giving feedback.
- Ask learners on what aspect of their vocabulary use they would like to have feedback and then tailor your feedback to those areas if it helps focus on the words.
- Record yourself giving feedback as you interview learners on their writing.[6] You could give the learners the recordings to review when they are rewriting their texts. Gardner[7] found that taping resulted in tutors providing more explicit and varied feedback.

■ Consider using a code system to indicate the vocabulary errors in the text.[8] For example:

Type of error	Code for vocabulary error
Wrong word	WW
Wrong meaning	WM
Spelling	SP
Wrong collocation	W/COLL.
Formality level	FORMAL/INFORMAL?
Word family	WF
Grammar	GR

If you do adopt a code, it is important to first to make sure that students know exactly what each symbol or abbreviation means. Then make sure they know what resources they may need to correct their errors. You might brainstorm a list of possible resources within your institution and community that learners could access for help with vocabulary error correction.

■ Ask learners to compare the first and second drafts of their writing to see if there are improvements and that they were made as a direct result of the feedback.

■ Reformulate parts of the text for students to model the language use or to clarify the meaning.[9] If you adopt this method, then it is important to allow time and opportunities for learners to work meaningfully with your feedback to ensure it is not lost.

- In feedback sessions, point out opportunities in the writing where academic words could naturally have been used instead of higher-frequency items. Make sure that using the academic vocabulary would improve the original or use the words productively.
- Use a feedback sheet that targets vocabulary use. The following is a small-scale example of a vocabulary feedback sheet.[10]

Aspect of vocabulary	Vocabulary errors in my text	Correction of errors
Meaning		
Collocations		
Spelling		
Choosing the right words		
Grammar and vocabulary		
Word families		
Other		

Learners record their vocabulary, analyse the problem, and then correct their errors. Make sure learners get to work on the vocabulary again, either with you directly or by rewriting the text using the codes to help them with corrections.

These opportunities for students to try out new language, get feedback on their attempts, and have another chance to try the language again are crucial for vocabulary acquisition and to increase learners' confidence.

Endnotes

1. For more on 'ear' learners, see Joy Reid's book in this series called *Essentials in teaching academic writing*.

2. I learned this technique from Paul Nation, School of Linguistics and Applied Language Studies, Victoria University of Wellington.

3. For more on writing development and academic vocabulary, see *Essentials of teaching academic writing* by Joy Reid and the writing books in this Houghton Mifflin series.

4. You can find an example of an information transfer activity on this book's website at http://www.college.hmco.com/esl/students.

5. Nation, P. 2001. *Learning vocabulary in another language*. Cambridge: Cambridge University Press. Page 183.

6. I first learned of this technique from Alastair Ker, School of Linguistics and Applied Language Studies, Victoria University of Wellington.

7. Gardner, S. 2004. Knock-on effects of mode change on academic discourse. *Journal of English for Academic Purposes 3*, 23–38. See especially page 36.

8. I first learned about coding systems at Victoria University of Wellington.

9. Jordan, R. 1997. *English for academic purposes*. Cambridge: Cambridge University Press. See especially page 175.

10. I first saw grammar-based error feedback sheets at the School of Linguistics and Applied Language Studies, Victoria University of Wellington. I have adapted this idea to focus on vocabulary.

Part **4**

Testing Academic Vocabulary

 16 Understanding Approaches to Testing Vocabulary

 17 Practical Techniques for Testing Academic Vocabulary

Chapter **16**

Understanding Approaches to Testing Vocabulary

This chapter provides some background ideas on testing vocabulary in general. We then move on to deciding what words to test and ways of testing recognition and recall. Then in Chapter 17, we look at testing vocabulary in writing and speaking.

Why Do We Test Academic Vocabulary?

We test the words learners know for several reasons. Some main purposes of vocabulary tests during a course could be to:

- Test how well learners are learning words over the long-term.
- Find out how well learners have just learned something.[1]
- Provide an incentive to study.[2] For some learners, however, test-taking anxiety can outweigh any incentive.
- Give learners an opportunity for developmental feedback on the form and meaning of the test words.
- Examine learners' vocabulary use to diagnose any problems to see whether they understand words they have met in new contexts.[3]

Other reasons for testing vocabulary include:

- Measuring the effectiveness of vocabulary-learning strategies.
- Placing learners in appropriate classes or courses.
- Assessing vocabulary size.[4]

What Do We Need to Keep in Mind When We Test Vocabulary?

We need to remember the major elements of successful tests: *validity*, *reliability*, and *practicality*.

Validity

- Is the test going to validly measure what your learners know about the target words?
- Does the test have a sufficient number of items in it? Nation[5] recommends a minimum of 30 words.

Reliability

- Does the test require learners to demonstrate knowledge of the vocabulary you are testing?[6]
- Will the test give consistent results no matter which student is taking it and which teacher is marking it?[7]

Practicality

- Is the test easy to prepare?
- Is it easy to mark?[8]
- Is the test an efficient measure of vocabulary? In other words, does the test take a long time to prepare and mark and for students to take? If so, is there a way to get the same information but in less time?

Some more questions to ask yourself about your vocabulary tests might be:

- Does the test have a good effect on learning and teaching?[9]
- Does the test provide motivation for learning words or is it something learners have to do to satisfy course requirements?
- Does the test actually test vocabulary? Some skills-based tests, such as reading or listening, may actually test language skill, rather than the learners' word knowledge.
- Are the test instructions more difficult than the test itself? If so, use high-frequency words in your test instructions.[10]
- Have you tried your test on colleagues? They might be able to offer some feedback on format and content.
- Have you tried the test on another group of learners? If it is a high-stakes test, you might want to try it with colleagues in a different institution to iron out any bugs before you give it to your students.[11]
- Is it possible that learners might get test items right without having to know the target vocabulary?[12] If learners have to match words and meanings, for example, you could include a few extra words or definitions as distractors.
- How often do you need to test?

What Words Should We Test?

The answer to this question depends on the purpose of your test.
Diagnostic, achievement and proficiency tests all measure different things.
Because this book's focus is academic vocabulary, we will concentrate on
testing these words. Basically, your vocabulary tests should focus on words
you have been working with in class. If these are the words in Sublist 1 of
the AWL, then you should test those words.

You could decide to focus on one AWL sublist per four weeks of class.
There are 60 words in Sublists 1–10, so students would focus on 15 words
per week. You could test different aspects of these words at the end of the
four weeks. As the teacher, you can decide what and how to test.

Another approach is for learners to select the words to be tested. In
this case, prepare the test so that each learner has an individual vocabulary
list but everyone can take the test. For example, if the test requires learners
to write several sentences using words in their individual lists, then learners
would select their own words to test.[13]

Here are some benefits to having learners select their own words
to test.

- Self-selecting words may help learners make learning decisions and
  develop autonomy.
- Learners are responsible for which words to learn and why so the
  class vocabulary learning programme becomes more individualised
  or personal.
- Students can choose to build their knowledge of partially known
  words to develop better comprehension or production.
- Principles of vocabulary learning can be put into practice. For
  example, learners need to know that they should choose to learn
  high-frequency words and this should influence their selection
  of words.

Some cautions apply to self-selection of vocabulary items however.

- Some learners may take some time to get used to choosing their own words for testing. One student in a colleague's class included the word *haberdashery* on his list, without realising the limited use and somewhat old-fashioned nature of the word.
- Moir and Nation,[14] in their study of strategy use by learners, reported that even when learners knew principles behind choosing which words to learn and how to learn them, reverted under test conditions to their old strategies and chose words they thought the teacher wanted them to learn.

What Aspects of Vocabulary Can We Test?

When we think about what aspects of vocabulary to test, the most obvious answer perhaps is to say we should test what learners have been learning during the course. A major focus might be making sure learners can use the words fluently and accurately in their writing. Another might be checking to see that learners know the meaning of words when used in a new context.[15]

Here are some aspects of knowing a word you might test:

- Form—spelling, word parts, written and spoken forms.
- Meaning—form and meaning, concepts, associations, collocations.
- Use—stress patterns, word families, collocations, and production in speaking and writing.[16]

In this chapter we looked at testing many aspects of knowing an academic word. Most of the assessment tasks are based on recognition and production through writing. Testing through speaking is a possibility but it is often part of a wider assessment in an academic presentation or seminar, for example, where vocabulary use in speaking is judged. Chapter 17 provides practical methods and tasks to assess knowledge of both spoken and written academic vocabulary.

Endnotes

1. Nation, P., and P. Meara. 2002. Vocabulary. In N. Schmitt, *An introduction to applied linguistics*. Arnold: London. See especially page 46.
2. Read, J. 2000. *Assessing vocabulary*. Cambridge: Cambridge University Press. Page 170.
3. Read, 2000. See especially page 152.
4. See Chapter 1 for details on the Vocabulary Levels Test.
5. Nation, P. 2001. *Learning vocabulary in another language*. Cambridge: Cambridge University Press. See especially page 345.
6. Nation, 2001. See especially page 345.
7. Thornbury, S. 2002. *How to teach vocabulary*. Harlow: Pearson Education. See especially pages 135–136.
8. Nation, 2001. See especially page 345.
9. Nation, 2001. See especially page 345.
10. Schmitt, N. 2000. *Vocabulary in language teaching*. Cambridge: Cambridge University Press. See especially page 172.
11. If you try the test somewhere else, you might consider how you can compensate students for their time. You could perhaps offer to go over answers or discuss vocabulary with them as feedback.
12. Read, 2000. See especially page 172.
13. Thank you to the English Proficiency Programme tutors in the School of Linguistics and Applied Language Studies, Victoria University of Wellington, New Zealand, for sharing this approach to vocabulary testing.
14. Moir, J., & I. S. P. Nation. 2002. Learners' use of strategies for effective vocabulary learning. *Prospect 17*(1), 15–35.
15. For further reading on testing, see Read, J. 2000. *Assessing vocabulary*. Cambridge: Cambridge University Press. You could also read the chapters on testing in Nation, 2001 and N. Schmitt. 2000. *Vocabulary in language teaching*. Cambridge: Cambridge University Press. See also Thornbury, S. 2002. *How to teach vocabulary*. Longman: Harlow, Essex.
16. Nation, 2001. See especially page 347.

Chapter 17

Practical Techniques for Testing Academic Vocabulary

- How can you test recognition and recall of academic vocabulary?
- How can you test your students' production of vocabulary?

This chapter builds on the ideas presented in Chapter 16 about testing knowledge of words. Here we look at testing vocabulary in writing and speaking.

How Can You Test Recognition and Recall of Academic Vocabulary?

■ **Matching meanings to words.**[1] For example:

definition	_____	1. a meaning
occurrence	_____	2. information
		3. something that has happened
		4. something that is needed

■ **True/false tests** whereby learners demonstrate their knowledge of a word's meaning through interpreting statements containing them. The example here is adapted from the true/false test of the first 1,000 words by Nation[2] and uses words from the AWL (in **bold**):

Are these statements true or false (T or F)?
A. _____ 2:1 is a **ratio.**
B. _____ These numbers are **odd:** 2, 4, 6, 8.
C. _____ This is a **sphere:** □

This format could be used for listening or reading.

■ **Collocations** using matching and generation exercises. For example:

Circle the words that are <u>common collocations</u> of *issue*.

visual	**global**	**complex**	**difficult**	**personal**	**yellow**

■ **Dictation.** Prepare a dictation text including the target words. The same text can be adapted to make a fill-in-the-blank or fill-in-the-phrase exercise. See Chapter 13 for examples of these exercises.
■ **Spelling.** Use academic vocabulary from your course in such activities as spelling bees and error correction tasks.

- **Accuracy of Word Use.** Supply sentences with the target words and ask students to correct where their use is not accurate.[3]
- **Word families.** Use words from the course.
  - Use a grid format to test knowledge of word family members and their parts of speech. You could add another column to elicit more word family members.

Word	Part of Speech	Family Word	Part of Speech
similar	*adjective*	similarity	*noun*
conflict			
assist			

  - Develop fill-in-the-blank tests with the correct word family form. For example:

1. The business went through a very rapid period of high growth and _____ (expand).

2. One important factor in a new position or job is whether the hours of work have some _____ (flexible).

- **Word Stress.** Use key words from your course.[4] For example, you could ask students to look at Sublists 1 and 2 of the AWL and write five (5) examples from the lists or their word families with the same stress patterns as the following words:

proceed	*period*	*theory*	*formulation*	*interpret*

- **Collocations.** Use academic words from your course. For example: Put a check mark (✓) in the box each time the word in the left column collocates with a word in the top row.

	problem	issue	factor	priority	project	potential
significant						
major						
enormous						

- **Word Associations.** See Read[5] for an explanation and examples of a word association test. This activity can help learners form a 'picture' of a word's use in the language. For example, which words would you associate with the word *assess*?[6]

language	federal	teacher	test	write	convert

How Can You Test Your Students' Production of Vocabulary?

Using a word in a sentence requires knowledge of collocations, parts of speech, meaning and register.[7] It is possible to see a range of vocabulary knowledge if you require learners to produce the target words in sentences or paragraphs.[8] You could use the same writing task at the start and at the end of the course and then analyze students' vocabulary use and accuracy to show progress.

- **Using words in context.** This could be done by speaking or writing individual sentences. For example:

Write a sentence with each of the following words, that shows you know the word's meaning and form. You can choose to use a family member of the words.

1. hence _____

2. integral _____

- **Paragraph writing.** See Chapter 15 for an example.
- **Essay writing.** You could assign an essay task on an academic topic and include a deliberate vocabulary focus by asking learners to try to use academic vocabulary focussed on in class.

Endnotes

1. This test is similar in format to the Vocabulary Levels Test (see Appendix 2).
2. This is an adaptation of the True/False test for the first 1,000 words in Appendix 2 of Nation, P. 2001. *Learning vocabulary in another language.* Cambridge: Cambridge University Press.
3. Nation, 2001. See especially page 353.
4. See *Essentials of teaching academic oral communication* by John Murphy and the *College oral communication* textbooks in this Houghton Mifflin series for more suggestions and exercises on vocabulary in speaking.
5. Read, J. 2000. *Assessing vocabulary.* Cambridge: Cambridge University Press. See especially page 181.
6. Nation, 2001. See especially page 353.
7. Schmitt, N. 2000. *Vocabulary in language teaching.* Cambridge: Cambridge University Press. See especially page 170.
8. Schmitt, 2000. See especially page 170.

Appendices

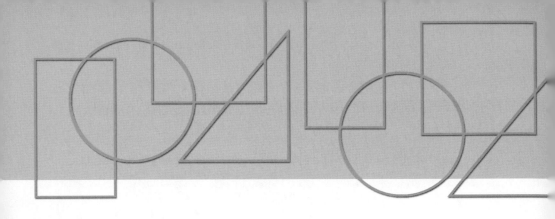

Sublists of the Academic Word List

Arranged by the frequency of word families in each sublist.

SUBLIST 1

require
income
section
structure
policy
economy
process
research
vary
issue
analyze
method
data
function
area
define
proceed
significant
individual
respond

identify
export
similar
approach
occur
environment
contract
involve
establish
specific
theory
benefit
major
assess
indicate
finance
evident
period
source
principle
percent

labour
consist
assume
factor
formula
legal
sector
authority
create
concept
constitute
legislate
distribute
derive
context
role
available
estimate
interpret

SUBLIST 2

range
obtain
strategy
conclude
commission
appropriate
institute
credit
region
acquire
invest
construct
community
design
item
equate
injure
chapter
participate
compute
select
relevant
maintain
reside
culture
text
regulate
final
distinct
potential
resource
element
administrate
focus
seek
achieve
site
consequent

survey
normal
complex
feature
consume
affect
primary
previous
secure
tradition
transfer
journal
conduct
purchase
positive
perceive
impact
evaluate
restrict
assist
category
aspect

SUBLIST 3

partner
technical
rely
corporate
contribute
exclude
react
sex
alternative
initial
convene
technology
circumstance
link
minor

comment
shift
sufficient
proportion
ensure
document
constant
component
core
immigrate
emphasis
valid
instance
consent
physical
fund
dominate
demonstrate
outcome
specify
volume
task
layer
maximise
technique
correspond
locate
framework
constrain
criteria
interact
illustrate
deduce
coordinate
compensate
imply
philosophy
negate
justify

scheme
sequence
publish
considerable
remove
register

SUBLIST 4

stress
statistic
concentrate
domestic
debate
subsequent
commit
mechanism
grant
professional
overall
hypothesis
investigate
summary
impose
civil
code
series
apparent
adequacy
ethnic
contrast
output
job
goal
cycle
internal
dimension
resolve
approximate
hence

principal
attitude
retain
promote
implement
sum
access
project
obvious
undertake
option
attribute
communicate
predict
occupy
confer
error
integrate
label
parameter
regime
prior
annual
despite
implicate
phase
status
parallel
emerge

SUBLIST 5

generate
target
clause
adjust
liberal
logic
licence
fundamental

image
generation
stable
expose
academy
orient
equivalent
external
mental
trend
enable
energy
sustain
style
transit
consult
compound
medical
welfare
whereas
objective
ratio
conflict
challenge
revenue
psychology
decline
aware
capacity
discrete
evolve
modify
symbol
contact
enforce
expand
precise
version
substitute

draft
notion
reject
entity
margin
facilitate
pursue
network
monitor
prime
amend
alter
perspective

SUBLIST 6

utilise
lecture
inhibit
rational
accuracy
explicit
assign
author
incorporate
reveal
minimum
acknowledge
underlie
trace
edit
cooperate
index
aggregate
transport
exceed
migrate
overseas
display
subsidy

incentive
presume
flexible
federal
domain
furthermore
ignorance
diverse
abstract
attach
nevertheless
scope
allocate
enhance
ministry
gender
tape
recover
neutral
incidence
input
fee
brief
intelligence
interval
expert
bond
transform
initiate
capable
precede
estate
motive
cite
discriminate
instruct

SUBLIST 7

release

deny
ultimate
adapt
differentiate
intervene
survive
innovate
advocate
simulate
file
isolate
unique
channel
paradigm
empirical
ideology
couple
media
chemical
confirm
dispose
infer
convert
finite
submit
mode
grade
dynamic
somewhat
quote
insert
phenomenon
transmit
thesis
reverse
identical
eliminate
sole
comprehensive

globe
classic
guarantee
foundation
equip
prohibit
contrary
aid
successor
topic
adult
extract
decade
hierarchy
priority
definite
voluntary
visible
publication
comprise

SUBLIST 8

accumulate
currency
schedule
detect
virtual
tense
displace
commodity
highlight
arbitrary
reinforce
appendix
paragraph
offset
intense
fluctuate
visual

predominant
terminate
exhibit
random
ambiguous
induce
uniform
chart
guideline
denote
radical
inspect
plus
abandon
deviate
appreciate
thereby
revise
implicit
eventual
bias
via
contradict
theme
practitioner
nuclear
inevitable
conform
exploit
accompany
vehicle
drama
crucial
contemporary
complement
clarify
manipulate
widespread
infrastructure

automate
restore
prospect
minimise

SUBLIST 9

vision
mediate
insight
controversy
restrain
accommodate
qualitative
anticipate
ethic
analogy
inherent
refine
temporary
mature
minimal
diminish
portion
duration
distort
intermediate
relax
behalf
sphere
team
norm
mutual
overlap
format
manual
preliminary
attain
unify
device

devote

bulk

assure

integral

found

military

route

confine

erode

coincide

suspend

subordinate

rigid

violate

cease

protocol

scenario

passive

revolution

concurrent

converse

commence

supplement

medium

coherent

trigger

compatible

SUBLIST 10

panel

persist

invoke

pose

incline

undergo

conceive

encounter

collapse

intrinsic

assemble

convince

reluctance

odd

notwithstanding

colleague

enormous

compile

depress

whereby

levy

nonetheless

integrity

adjacent

ongoing

albeit

so-called

straightforward

likewise

forthcoming

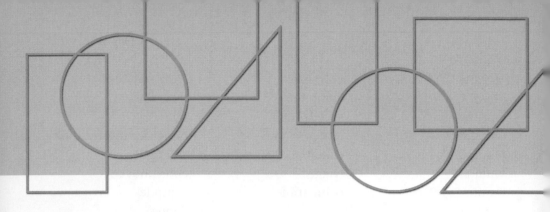

A Vocabulary Levels Test: Version 2[1]

This is a vocabulary test. You must choose the right word to go with each meaning. Write the number of that word next to its meaning. Here is an example.

1	business	_____	part of a house
2	clock	_____	animal with four legs
3	horse	_____	something used for writing
4	pencil		
5	shoe		
6	wall		

You answer it in the following way.

1	business	_6_	part of a house
2	clock	_3_	animal with four legs
3	horse	_4_	something used for writing
4	pencil		
5	shoe		
6	wall		

Some words are in the test to make it more difficult. You do not have to find a meaning for these words. In the example above, these words are *business*, *clock*, *shoe*. Try to do every part of the test.

Version 2 The 2,000 word level

1	copy	_____	end or highest point
2	event	_____	this moves a car
3	motor	_____	thing made to be like another
4	pity		
5	profit		
6	tip		

1	accident	_____	loud deep sound
2	debt	_____	something you must pay
3	fortune	_____	having a high opinion of yourself
4	pride		
5	roar		
6	thread		

1	coffee	_____	money for work
2	disease	_____	a piece of clothing
3	justice	_____	using the law in the right way
4	skirt		
5	stage		
6	wage		

1	clerk	_____	a drink
2	frame	_____	office worker
3	noise	_____	unwanted sound
4	respect		
5	theatre		
6	wine		

1	dozen	_____	chance
2	empire	_____	twelve
3	gift	_____	money paid to the government
4	opportunity		
5	relief		
6	tax		

1	admire	_____	make wider or longer
2	complain	_____	bring in for the first time
3	fix	_____	have a high opinion of someone
4	hire		
5	introduce		
6	stretch		

1	arrange	_____	grow
2	develop	_____	put in order
3	lean	_____	like more than something else
4	owe		
5	prefer		
6	seize		

1	blame	_____	make
2	elect	_____	choose by voting
3	jump	_____	become like water
4	manufacture		
5	melt		
6	threaten		

1	ancient	_____	not easy
2	curious	_____	very old
3	difficult	_____	related to God
4	entire		
5	holy		
6	social		

1	bitter	_____	beautiful
2	independent	_____	small
3	lovely	_____	liked by many people
4	merry		
5	popular		
6	slight		

Version 2 The 3,000 word level

1	bull	_____	formal and serious manner
2	champion	_____	winner of a sporting event
3	dignity	_____	building where valuable objects are shown
4	hell		
5	museum		
6	solution		

1	blanket	_____	holiday
2	contest	_____	good quality
3	generation	_____	wool covering used on beds
4	merit		
5	plot		
6	vacation		

1	comment	_____	long formal dress
2	gown	_____	goods from a foreign country
3	import	_____	part of the body which carries feeling
4	nerve		
5	pasture		
6	tradition		

1	administration	_____	group of animals
2	angel	_____	spirit who serves God
3	fort	_____	managing business and affairs
4	frost		
5	herd		
6	pond		

1	atmosphere	_____	advice
2	counsel	_____	a place covered with grass
3	factor	_____	female chicken
4	hen		
5	lawn		
6	muscle		

1	abandon	_____ live in a place
2	dwell	_____ live in a place
3	oblige	_____ leave something permanently
4	pursue	
5	quote	
6	resolve	

1	assemble	_____ look closely
2	attach	_____ stop doing something
3	peer	_____ cry out loudly in fear
4	quit	
5	scream	
6	toss	

1	drift	_____ suffer patiently
2	endure	_____ join wool threads together
3	grasp	_____ hold firmly with your hands
4	knit	
5	register	
6	tumble	

1	brilliant	_____ thin
2	distinct	_____ steady
3	magic	_____ without clothes
4	naked	
5	slender	
6	stable	

1	aware	_____ usual
2	blank	_____ best or most important
3	desperate	_____ knowing what is happening
4	normal	
5	striking	
6	supreme	

Version 2 The 5,000 word level

1	analysis	_____	eagerness
2	curb	_____	loan to buy a house
3	gravel	_____	small stones mixed with sand
4	mortgage		
5	scar		
6	zeal		

1	cavalry	_____	small hill
2	eve	_____	day or night before a holiday
3	ham	_____	soldiers who fight from horses
4	mound		
5	steak		
6	switch		

1	circus	_____	musical instrument
2	jungle	_____	seat without a back or arms
3	nomination	_____	speech given by a priest in a church
4	sermon		
5	stool		
6	trumpet		

1	artillery	_____	a kind of tree
2	creed	_____	system of belief
3	hydrogen	_____	large gun on wheels
4	maple		
5	pork		
6	streak		

1	chart	_____	map
2	forge	_____	large beautiful house
3	mansion	_____	place where metals are made and shaped
4	outfit		
5	sample		
6	volunteer		

1   contemplate   _____ think about deeply
2   extract   _____ bring back to health
3   gamble   _____ make someone angry
4   launch
5   provoke
6   revive

---

1   demonstrate   _____ have a rest
2   embarrass   _____ break suddenly into small pieces
3   heave   _____ make someone feel shy or nervous
4   obscure
5   relax
6   shatter

---

1   correspond   _____ exchange letters
2   embroider   _____ hide and wait for someone
3   lurk   _____ feel angry about something
4   penetrate
5   prescribe
6   resent

---

1   decent   _____ weak
2   frail   _____ concerning a city
3   harsh   _____ difficult to believe
4   incredible
5   municipal
6   specific

---

1   adequate   _____ enough
2   internal   _____ fully grown
3   mature   _____ alone away from other things
4   profound
5   solitary
6   tragic

Version 2 Academic Vocabulary

1	area	_____	written agreement
2	contract	_____	way of doing something
3	definition	_____	reason for believing something is or is
4	evidence		not true
5	method		
6	role		

1	debate	_____	plan
2	exposure	_____	choice
3	integration	_____	joining something into a whole
4	option		
5	scheme		
6	stability		

1	access	_____	male or female
2	gender	_____	study of the mind
3	implementation	_____	entrance or way in
4	license		
5	orientation		
6	psychology		

1	accumulation	_____	collecting things over time
2	edition	_____	promise to repair a broken product
3	guarantee	_____	feeling a strong reason or need to do
4	media		something
5	motivation		
6	phenomenon		

1	adult	_____	end
2	exploitation	_____	machine used to move people or goods
3	infastructure	_____	list of things to do at certain times
4	schedule		
5	termination		
6	vehicle		

1	alter	_____ change
2	coincide	_____ say something is not true
3	deny	_____ describe clearly and exactly
4	devote	
5	release	
6	specify	

1	correspond	_____ keep
2	diminish	_____ match or be in agreement with
3	emerge	_____ give special attention to something
4	highlight	
5	invoke	
6	retain	

1	bond	_____ make smaller
2	channel	_____ guess the number or size of something
3	estimate	_____ recognizing and naming a person or thing
4	identify	
5	mediate	
6	minimise	

1	explicit	_____ last
2	final	_____ stiff
3	negative	_____ meaning 'no' or 'not'
4	professional	
5	rigid	
6	sole	

1	abstract	_____ next to
2	adjacent	_____ added to
3	controversial	_____ concerning the whole world
4	global	
5	neutral	
6	supplementary	

Version 2 The 10,000 word level

1	alabaster	_____	small barrel
2	chandelier	_____	soft white stone
3	dogma	_____	tool for shaping wood
4	keg		
5	rasp		
6	tentacle		

1	benevolence	_____	kindness
2	convoy	_____	set of musical notes
3	lien	_____	speed control for an engine
4	octave		
5	stint		
6	throttle		

1	bourgeois	_____	middle class people
2	brocade	_____	row or level of something
3	consonant	_____	cloth with a pattern of gold or silver threads
4	prelude		
5	stupor		
6	tier		

1	alcove	_____	priest
2	impetus	_____	release from prison early
3	maggot	_____	medicine to put on wounds
4	parole		
5	salve		
6	vicar		

1	alkali	_____	light joking talk
2	banter	_____	a rank of British nobility
3	coop	_____	picture made of small pieces of glass
4	mosaic		or stone
5	stealth		
6	viscount		

1	dissipate	_____	steal
2	flaunt	_____	scatter or vanish
3	impede	_____	twist the body about uncomfortably
4	loot		
5	squirm		
6	vie		

1	contaminate	_____	write carelessly
2	cringe	_____	move back because of fear
3	immerse	_____	put something under water
4	peek		
5	relay		
6	scrawl		

1	blurt	_____	walk in a proud way
2	dabble	_____	kill by squeezing someone's throat
3	dent	_____	say suddenly without thinking
4	pacify		
5	strangle		
6	swagger		

1	illicit	_____	immense
2	lewd	_____	against the law
3	mammoth	_____	wanting revenge
4	slick		
5	temporal		
6	vindictive		

1	indolent	_____	lazy
2	nocturnal	_____	no longer used
3	obsolete	_____	clever and tricky
4	torrid		
5	translucent		
6	wily		

Endnotes

1. Thank you to Norbert Schmitt for permission to include this test here. Another version of the test is available in Schmitt, N. (2000). *Vocabulary in language teaching.* Cambridge: Cambridge University Press.

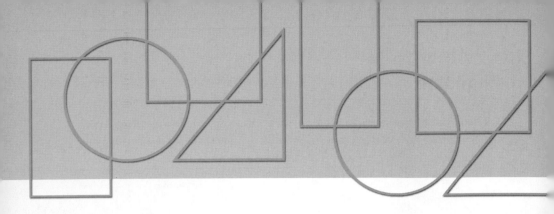

Appendix **3**

Top Ten Resources

Printed Publications

Coady, J. & T. Huckin. (Eds.). 1997. *Second language vocabulary acquisition.* Cambridge: Cambridge University Press.

Folse, K. 2004. *Vocabulary myths.* Ann Arbor: University of Michigan Press.

Leech, G., P. Rayson & A. Wilson. 2001. *Word frequencies in written and spoken English.* Harlow, Essex: Longman.

Lewis, M. 2000. (Ed.). *Teaching collocation: Further developments in the lexical approach.* Hove: Language Teaching Publications.

Nation, I.S.P. 2001. *Learning vocabulary in another language.* Cambridge: Cambridge University Press.

Read, J. 2000. *Assessing vocabulary.* Cambridge: Cambridge University Press.

Schmitt, N. 2000. *Vocabulary in language teaching.* Cambridge: Cambridge University Press.

Schmitt, N. & M. McCarthy. (Eds). 1997. *Vocabulary: Description, acquisition and pedagogy.* Cambridge: Cambridge University Press.

Singleton, D. 2000. *Language and the lexicon.* London: Arnold.

Thornbury, S. 2002. *How to teach vocabulary.* Harlow, Essex: Longman.

Websites

Many vocabulary websites have already been developed; others are being added on a regular basis. An up-to-date list is maintained on the Houghton Mifflin website for this book at http://www.college.hmco.com/esl/instructors.

Index